# Building Better Behaviour in the EarlyYears

Chris Dukes and Maggie Smith

SAGE

Los Angeles | London | New Delhi
Singapore | Washington DC

SAGE Publications Ltd
1 Oliver's Yard
55 City Road
London EC1Y 1SP

SAGE Publications Inc.
2455 Teller Road
Thousand Oaks, California 91320

SAGE Publications India Pvt Ltd
B 1/I 1 Mohan Cooperative Industrial Area
Mathura Road
New Delhi 110 044

SAGE Publications Asia-Pacific Pte Ltd
33 Pekin Street #02-01
Far East Square
Singapore 048763

Library of Congress Control Number: 2008934471

British Library Cataloguing in Publication data

A catalogue record for this book is available from the British Library

ISBN 978-1-84787-519-8
ISBN 978-1-84787-520-4(pbk)

Typeset by C&M Digitals (P) Ltd, Chennai, India
Printed in India by Replika Press Pvt. Ltd.
Printed on paper from sustainable resources

Contents

Acknowledgements

This book is dedicated to Eithne Leming and SallyAnn Hart who have inspired and taught us so much.

About the authors

Chris Dukes is a qualified teacher with over 20 years' experience. She has worked in various London primary schools as a class teacher and later as a member of the Senior Management Team. Chris has a Masters degree in Special Needs and through her later roles as a SENCO and support teacher, many years' experience of working with children with a variety of needs. Chris has worked closely with staff teams, mentoring, advising and supervising work with children with additional needs, as well as with other education and health professionals. Chris currently works as an Area SENCO supporting Special Needs Coordinators and managers in a wide range of pre-school settings. As well as advising she writes courses, delivers training and produces publications.

Maggie Smith began her career as a nursery teacher in Birmingham. She has worked as a peri-patetic teacher for an under-5s EAL Team and went on to become the Foundation Stage manager of an Early Years Unit in Inner London. Maggie helped to set up an innovative unit for young children with behavioural difficulties and has also worked supporting families of children with special needs. She has taught on Early Years BTEC and CACHE courses at a college of higher education. She currently works as an Area SENCO supporting Special Needs Coordinators and managers in a wide range of pre-school settings. As well as advising she writes courses, delivers training and produces publications.

Contents of the CD-ROM

How to use the CD-ROM

The CD-ROM contains pdf files of the worksheets from this book organised by chapter. You will need Acrobat Reader version 3 or higher to view and print these pages.

The documents are set to print at A4 but you can enlarge them to A3 by increasing the output percentage using the page set-up settings for your printer.

Throughout the book, you will see this CD icon used ✪. This indicates that the material you are looking at is also available electronically on the accompanying CD-ROM.

Contents of the CD-ROM

Chapter 5

Chapter 6

Chapter 7

Introduction

Our starting point for this book is that behaviour should be viewed in the same way as any other area of the early years curriculum. Children need to be shown and supported in how to develop better behaviour by the adults around them, and behaviour cannot be separated from a child's personal, social and emotional development.

In writing this book we have set out to illustrate that:

▶ issues around behaviour are complex and can evoke strong feelings;

▶ there is rarely a single answer or a magic wand to resolve difficulties;

▶ settings which have built better behaviour are those which are able to look at each child holistically and are reflective about themselves and their environment;

▶ when practitioners are able to be reflective they can create a setting that is proactive and positive about behaviour;

▶ practitioners with a 'can do' attitude feel confident that they can guide and support children to develop better behaviour;

▶ there are some key strategies, skills and resources which will help to build better behaviour.

This book will invaluable to:

▶ **Pre-school practitioners**

This book will enable you to develop your knowledge and understanding of children's behaviour. You will be supported by practical examples and strategies to use within your setting. The Hands-on activities will provide a starting point for team discussion.

▶ **Tutors and students**

This book will increase your awareness of issues surrounding behaviour. It will provide a starting point for building on your own current and future practice. The Hands-on activities can be used as short assignments.

▶ **Advisers**

Use this book to support pre-schools to build better behaviour. The strategies and skills banks particularly can be used for staff training and the chapters on the holistic child and the reflective setting are an excellent starting point for whole-team development.

A note on the text

The case studies included in this publication are a composite of numerous children in various settings distilled from the authors' many years of experience. They are not specific to any one child, practitioner or setting.

Poem

So It Is With Behaviour

Learning to behave is a bit like learning to ride a bicycle.
No child is born knowing how to ride a bike but some have more aptitude for it than others and some catch on quite quickly.
Other children have to persevere and be shown over and over again or have to have someone running alongside to steady them.
So it is with behaviour.

While they are learning they may need the extra support of three wheels or stabilisers before they have the confidence to try on two wheels.
They often wobble and lose their balance; sometimes they fall off and have to start over again.
Even when they feel they have mastered it, they might find themselves on unfamiliar roads or uneven surfaces which can make them wobble and fall off all over again.
So it is with behaviour.

So every cycle ride is something of a trial and error – they never quite know what they will encounter or how well they will coordinate the steering and pedalling and they still need someone to help them along the right path.
So it is with behaviour.

Practitioners and parents are like the extra wheels or stabilisers on the bicycle.
They keep children steady until they are ready to try to balance by themselves.
As children become more confident adults can step back a little but are still alongside them to help them when they make a mistake, forget what they have been taught or encounter a difficult path.
So it is with behaviour.

By Chris Dukes and Maggie Smith

CHAPTER ONE

The bigger picture

The aim of this chapter is to put children's behaviour into the wider context.

It outlines the references made to behaviour and behaviour management in the following documents:

▶ The Early Years Foundation Stage – Statutory Framework (DfES, 2007)

▶ The Early Years Foundation Stage – Practice Guidance (DfES, 2008)

▶ The Code of Practice for Special Educational Needs (DfEE, 2001)

▶ The Disability Discrimination Act (NCB, 1995)

and includes:

▶ a Hands-on activity

▶ Further reading.

Most practitioners would agree that a positive attitude, self-esteem and good behaviour are essential for children to develop and learn successfully. The importance of children's personal, social and emotional development is highlighted in recent initiatives and is embedded in the EYFS. Both the Statutory Framework and the non-statutory Practice Guidance make reference to behaviour, the main points of which are listed below. These may be particularly helpful to managers and those responsible for behaviour management and training within a setting.

The Statutory Framework for the EYFS

Welfare requirements

Safeguarding and promoting children's welfare

Children's behaviour must be managed effectively and in a manner appropriate for their stage of development and particular individual needs.

(EYFS Statutory Framework, page 25)

Specific legal requirements

Providers must not give corporal punishment to a child for whom they provide early years provision and, so far as it is reasonably practicable, shall ensure that corporal punishment is not given to any such child by:

▶ any person who cares for, or who is in regular contact with children;

▶ any person living or working on the premises.

Providers must not threaten corporal punishment or use or threaten any form of corporal punishment which could have an adverse impact on a child's well-being.

Providers must have an effective **behaviour management policy** which is adhered to by all members of staff.

Statutory guidance to which providers must have regard

A **named practitioner** should be responsible for behaviour management issues. They should be supported in acquiring skills to provide guidance to other staff and to access expert advice if ordinary methods are not effective with a particular child.

Physical intervention should only be used to manage a child's behaviour if it is necessary to prevent personal injury to the child, other children or an adult, to prevent serious damage to property or in what would reasonably be regarded as exceptional circumstances.

Any occasion where physical intervention is used to manage a child's behaviour should be recorded and parents should be informed about it on the same day.

Practice Guidance for the EYFS

The EYFS Practice Guidance looks at how practitioners can support the learning, development and welfare of all children. It is written to correspond with the principles which are divided into four themes:

▶ A Unique Child

▶ Positive Relationships

▶ Enabling Environments

▶ Learning and Development.

These themes underpin effective practice in the delivery of the EYFS (Practice Guidance, page 5).

Most references to behaviour are found in one of the Six Areas of Learning – that of Personal, Social and Emotional Development.

In particular it says that practitioners should:

> **Give support and a structured approach to vulnerable children and those with particular behavioural or communication difficulties to help them achieve successful Personal, Social and Emotional Development.**
>
> (EYFS Practice Guidance, page 25)

A child's behaviour is rooted in their personal, social and emotional development, which is helpfully set out in the EYFS Practice Guidance, page 24, as follows:

▶ For children, being special to someone and well cared for is vital for their physical, social and emotional health and well-being.

▶ Being acknowledged and affirmed by important people in their lives leads to children gaining confidence and inner strength through secure attachments with these people.

▶ Exploration within close relationships leads to growth of self-assurance, promoting a sense of belonging which allows children to explore the world from a secure base.

▶ Children need adults to set a good example and to give them opportunities for interaction with others so that they can develop positive ideas about themselves and others.

▶ Children who are encouraged to feel free to express their ideas and their feelings, such as joy, sadness, frustration and fear, can develop strategies to cope with new, challenging or stressful situations.

When does behaviour become a special need?

The Special Educational Needs Code of Practice

The SEN Code of Practice (DfEE, 2001) outlines certain expectations with regard to identifying and meeting the needs of children with learning difficulties and/or disabilities. These include a series of principles that early years settings are expected to adhere to.

The principles of the SEN Code of Practice are as follows:

▶ Every child with special educational needs should have their needs met.

▶ As far as possible these needs will be met within a mainstream setting with access to a broad, balanced and relevant curriculum.

▶ The views of parents should be sought and taken into account.

▶ Wherever possible the views of the child should be, taken into account.

(DfEE, 2001: 16, para. 2:2)

The SEN Code of Practice describes **special educational needs** as falling into four main areas:

▶ Communication and interaction

▶ Cognition and learning

▶ *Behavioural, emotional and social development*

▶ Sensory and physical.

The legal definition of SEN (Education Act 1996) as set out in the SEN Code of Practice (DfEE, 2001: 6, para. 1:3) is:

Children have special educational needs if they have a *learning difficulty* which calls for *special educational provision* to be made for them.

Children have a *learning difficulty* if they:

(a) have a significantly greater difficulty than the majority of children of the same age; or

(b) have a disability which prevents or hinders them from making use of the educational facilities to be found locally for children of the same age

(c) are under compulsory school age and fall within the definition at (a) or (b) above or would do so if special educational provision was not made for them.

Some children with challenging behaviour could therefore be described as having a special educational need.

Policies and procedures

The SEN Code of Practice sets out very clearly the procedures to be followed once a child is identified as having special or additional needs. The importance of both parental involvement and child participation is a key principle in this process.

The actions which follow are called a ***graduated response***.

All practitioners are expected to put in place systems and strategies to support children's behaviour. The trigger for deciding that extra support or intervention is needed is described as when a child presents:

> *... persistent emotional and/or behavioural difficulties which are not ameliorated by the behaviour management techniques usually employed in the setting.*

Practitioners would be expected to follow the guidance and graduated response outlined in the SEN Code of Practice. The child would be said to be at ***Early Years Action*** and the setting would be expected to work closely with parents. Targets would be recorded on a behaviour support plan or an individual education plan, which would be monitored and regularly reviewed. More information about this can be found in Chapter 6.

If targeted interventions, which are 'additional to or different from' what is normally available for children in the setting, are still unsuccessful after an agreed period of time, then the early years setting may wish to seek outside help. The trigger for seeking help from outside agencies could be that despite receiving an individualised programme and/or concentrated support:

> *... the child has emotional or behavioural difficulties which substantially and regularly interfere with the child's own learning or that of the group, despite having an individualised behaviour management programme.*

Again the setting would be expected to work closely with parents and outside agencies to write an individual education plan or behaviour support plan. The child would be said to be at ***Early Years Action Plus***.

For a very small number of children even this level of support might not be enough to help them make adequate progress and a Statutory Assessment would be requested to obtain a Statement of Educational Need. Early Years settings would always be supported by local authority advisers at this stage.

Roles and responsibilities

The SEN Code of Practice assigns the day-to-day organisation and coordination of special needs provision to the Special Educational Needs Coordinator (SENCO). However, it also clearly states that identification of, planning for and working with children with special needs, learning difficulties and disabilities – including those with behavioural needs – lies firmly with *all* members of staff.

Other legislation relevant to children's behaviour

The Disability Discrimination Act 1995

The Disability Discrimination Act 1995 (DDA) and subsequent disability legislation are relevant to a wide range of early years providers. It raises some questions as to whether or not children with behavioural difficulties are included in the definition of 'disabled' as described in the DDA.

It seems that there are certain circumstances when this would be the case:

> *A child may have significant behavioural difficulties and these may relate to an underlying impairment. If they do, the child may count as disabled because of the underlying impairment.*

A child displaying behavioural difficulties with an underlying impairment such as autism or severe speech, language or communication difficulties, for example, could therefore be described as disabled. They are therefore protected under the DDA.

The DDA sets out two *core duties*:

> 1. *Not to treat a disabled child* **less favourably.**
> 2. *To make* **reasonable adjustments** *for disabled children.*
>
> From October 2004 'reasonable adjustments' includes removing physical barriers.
>
> The core duties are *anticipatory* and provision and plans for disabled children should therefore be in place before they might actually be needed.

The DDA has implications for all aspects of the policies and practice of early years settings and also sits well alongside the principles of the EYFS.

Settings should note the need to include in their equal opportunities policies information about how reasonable adjustments will be made to cater for individual needs.

The anticipatory nature of these duties also means that settings will need to be aware of what *might* be needed and plan for future eventualities.

Hands-on activity

Look at the Practice Guidance for the EYFS, page 24: Personal, Social and Emotional Development.

How does the EYFS suggest that settings can effectively implement this area of learning and development?

 Further reading

Department for Education and Employment (2001) *Special Educational Needs: Code of Practice*. DfEE.

Department for Education and Skills (2007) *Statutory Framework for the Early Years Foundation Stage*. DfES.

Department for Education and Skills (2008) *Practice Guidance for the Early Years Foundation Stage*. DfES.

National Children's Bureau Enterprise Ltd (2003) *Early Years and the Disability Discrimination Act 1995: What Service Providers Need to Know*. NCB.

CHAPTER TWO

Development matters

This chapter aims to give practitioners some guidance on what to expect of a child in terms of their behaviour according to their age and stage of development, set within the context of their personal, social and emotional development.

It sets out some common behaviour characteristics and some ideas for practitioners to try for children in the following ages or stages of development:

▶ 16–26 months

▶ 22–36 months

▶ 30–50 months

▶ 40–60+ months

and includes:

▶ a Hands-on activity

▶ Further reading.

The aim of all pre-schools is to establish a safe and caring environment that supports and encourages children's learning as well as their personal growth. A consequence of this wonderfully rich environment is that children will feel free to try out new things, experiment and express their feelings. This is natural and is a credit to the practitioners who have put in so much effort to creating it.

The Early Years Foundation Stage acknowledges this and states that:

Children who are encouraged to feel free to express their ideas and their feelings, such as joy, sadness, frustration and fear, can develop strategies to cope with new, challenging or stressful situations.

(EYFS Practice Guidance, page 24)

In short, practitioners should not expect children to attend their settings with perfect behaviours already in place. As in any other area of child development, children need to learn how to develop satisfying relationships and manage their own feelings and resulting behaviours, and as in all other areas of development, some find this easier than others.

Behaviour 'lapses' should be regarded as natural and part of the pattern of child development. This does not mean, however, that a child's excesses should be sanctioned or encouraged by practitioners, but merely that practitioners should use their common sense and knowledge of child development to support a child to move on from a behaviour pattern.

Just as with any other area of development practitioners need to have realistic expectations of children's behaviour at specific ages and stages. The EYFS Practice Guidance (pages 26–36) identifies four particular areas of behavioural development which can be supported:

▶ Dispositions and Attitudes

▶ Self-confidence and Self-esteem

▶ Making Relationships

▶ Behaviour and Self-control.

The following diagrams, which begin at 16 months, can be used to remind you of the types of behaviour that *may be* usual for children at specific ages and stages.
For each age or stage of development:

▶ the diagrams on the left-hand pages show *some common behaviour characteristics* and use the developmental ages or stages outlined in the EYFS;

▶ the diagrams on the right-hand pages are linked to the same ages and stages and contain some *ideas to try.*

Note that not all children will exhibit these behaviour traits. The diagrams only contain examples of behaviours and are not exhaustive.

Some Common Behaviour Characteristics
16–26 Months

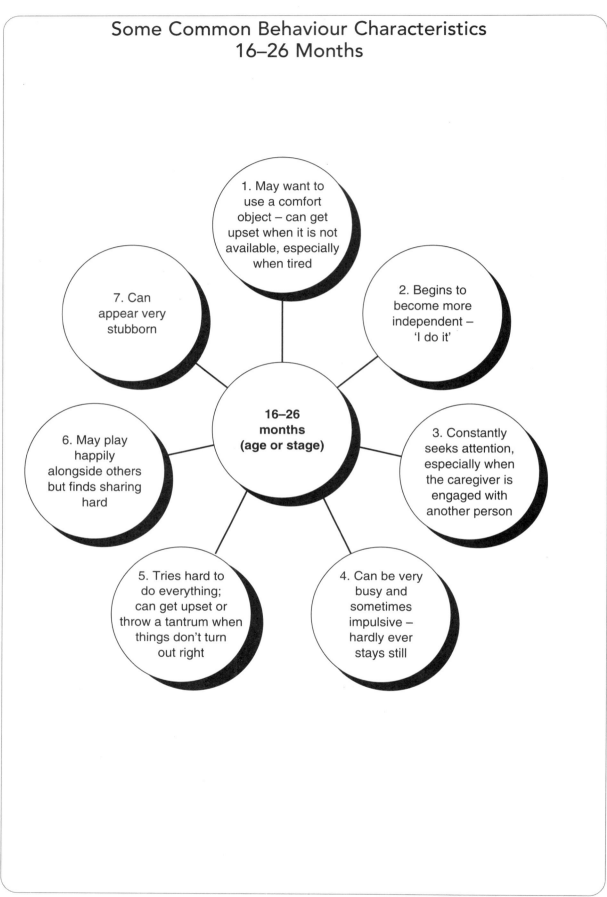

1. May want to use a comfort object – can get upset when it is not available, especially when tired

2. Begins to become more independent – 'I do it'

3. Constantly seeks attention, especially when the caregiver is engaged with another person

4. Can be very busy and sometimes impulsive – hardly ever stays still

5. Tries hard to do everything; can get upset or throw a tantrum when things don't turn out right

6. May play happily alongside others but finds sharing hard

7. Can appear very stubborn

16–26 months (age or stage)

Ideas to Try
16–26 Months

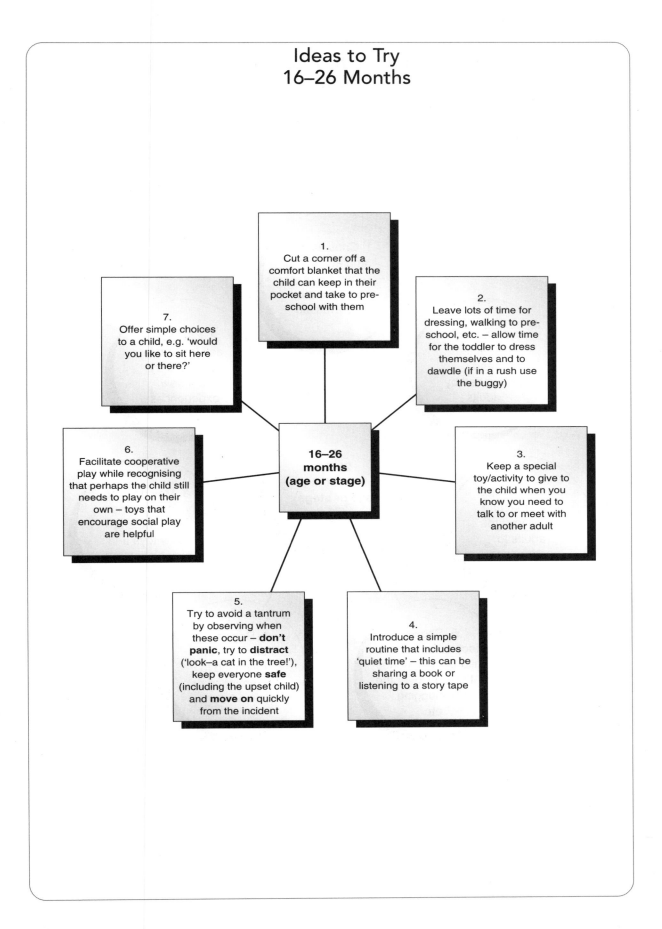

1.
Cut a corner off a comfort blanket that the child can keep in their pocket and take to pre-school with them

2.
Leave lots of time for dressing, walking to pre-school, etc. – allow time for the toddler to dress themselves and to dawdle (if in a rush use the buggy)

7.
Offer simple choices to a child, e.g. 'would you like to sit here or there?'

16–26 months (age or stage)

3.
Keep a special toy/activity to give to the child when you know you need to talk to or meet with another adult

6.
Facilitate cooperative play while recognising that perhaps the child still needs to play on their own – toys that encourage social play are helpful

5.
Try to avoid a tantrum by observing when these occur – **don't panic**, try to **distract** ('look–a cat in the tree!'), keep everyone **safe** (including the upset child) and **move on** quickly from the incident

4.
Introduce a simple routine that includes 'quiet time' – this can be sharing a book or listening to a story tape

Some Common Behaviour Characteristics
22–36 Months

1. Cries easily and at times may seem sensitive or embarrassed

2. Can push self forward in a rush to try out new experiences

3. May develop a strong sense of ownership over toys and play equipment

4. Begins to take turns but may need to be reminded or shown how to

5. Shows affection for younger children and friends but can be 'over the top', hugging, etc.

6. May develop fears that can be difficult for adults to understand

7. Can be distracted and persuaded by adults

22–36 months (age or stage)

Ideas to Try
22–36 Months

1.
Be sensitive to a child's feelings – never laugh at (even in a good humoured way) or draw attention to a child's discomfort

2.
Create a sense of order when introducing new equipment or experiences to young children. Talk and prepare them first, agreeing ground rules. Minimise waiting time

7.
Anticipate times of stress for a child and distract them with other activities or by asking for their help

22–36 months (age or stage)

3.
Discourage children from bringing their own toys into pre-school and try to create a sense of community and joint ownership of nursery equipment

6.
Acknowledge a child's fears without 'talking it up' – take the 'panic' out of a fear by talking about it in a normal way and saying that everyone gets scared some of the time. Discuss strategies with parents

5.
Role model friendship and appropriate physical contact with colleagues as well as with the children

4.
Support children's efforts to share but don't expect them to be able to do this all the time. Provide a balance of activities and enough equipment

Some Common Behaviour Characteristics
30–50 Months

1. Beginning to understand clear boundaries but will sometimes push to limits

2. Beginning to understand consequences of actions and how their actions affect others

30–50 months (age or stage)

3. Can share and take turns but may still need support especially when engrossed in play

4. Is aware of social approval or disapproval

5. Sometimes uses actions and words that they have seen displayed by older siblings or on TV

6. Empathy should be developing fast – beginning to see and accept others' points of view

7. Fights or quarrels with playmates and peers usually over play equipment or roles in imaginative play

Ideas to Try
30–50 Months

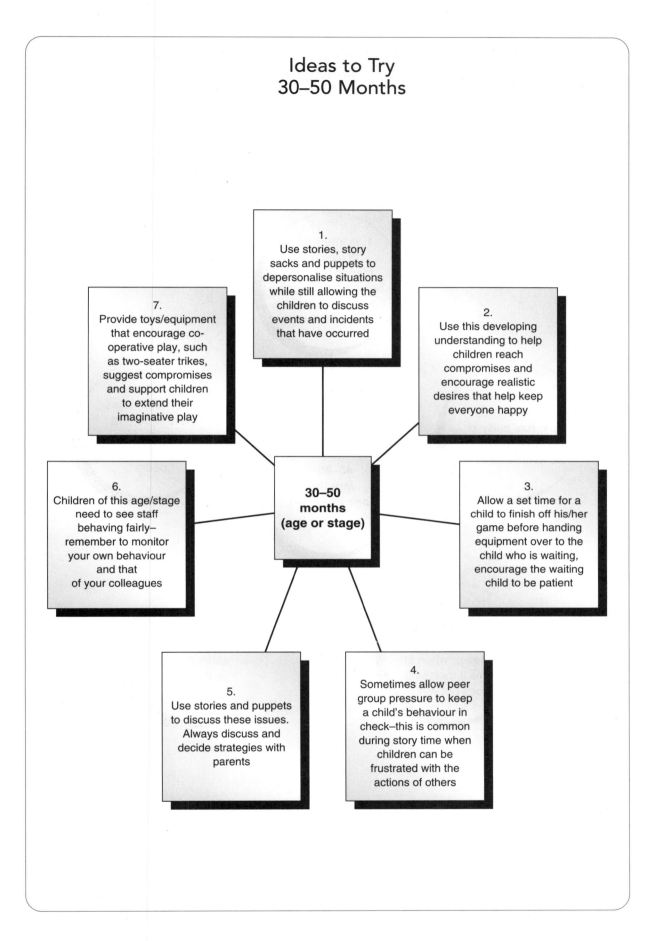

1.
Use stories, story sacks and puppets to depersonalise situations while still allowing the children to discuss events and incidents that have occurred

2.
Use this developing understanding to help children reach compromises and encourage realistic desires that help keep everyone happy

3.
Allow a set time for a child to finish off his/her game before handing equipment over to the child who is waiting, encourage the waiting child to be patient

4.
Sometimes allow peer group pressure to keep a child's behaviour in check–this is common during story time when children can be frustrated with the actions of others

5.
Use stories and puppets to discuss these issues. Always discuss and decide strategies with parents

6.
Children of this age/stage need to see staff behaving fairly– remember to monitor your own behaviour and that of your colleagues

7.
Provide toys/equipment that encourage co-operative play, such as two-seater trikes, suggest compromises and support children to extend their imaginative play

30–50 months (age or stage)

Some Common Behaviour Characteristics
40–60+ Months

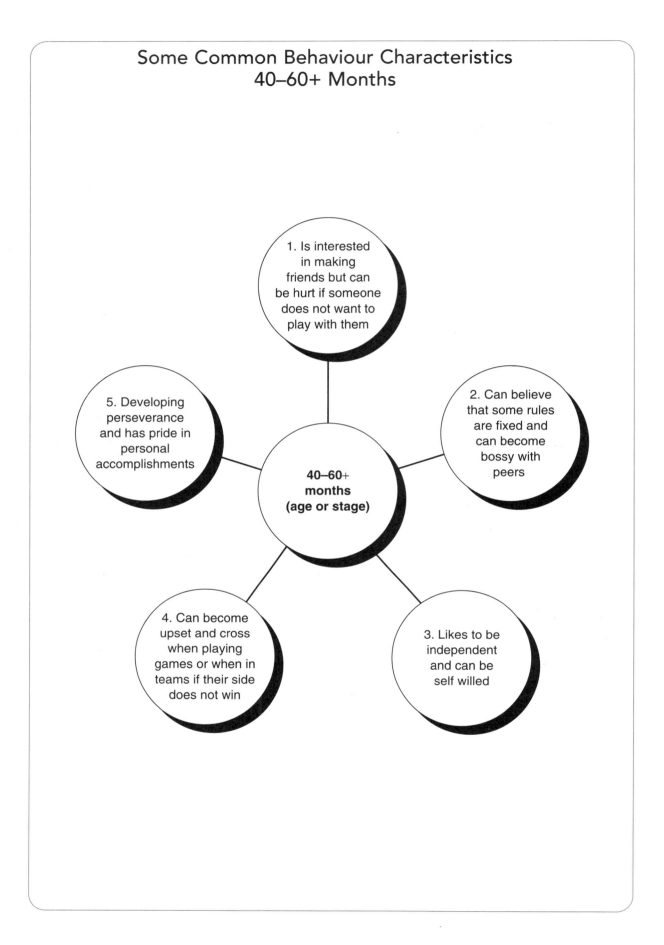

1. Is interested in making friends but can be hurt if someone does not want to play with them

5. Developing perseverance and has pride in personal accomplishments

40–60+ months (age or stage)

2. Can believe that some rules are fixed and can become bossy with peers

4. Can become upset and cross when playing games or when in teams if their side does not win

3. Likes to be independent and can be self willed

Ideas to Try
40–60+ Months

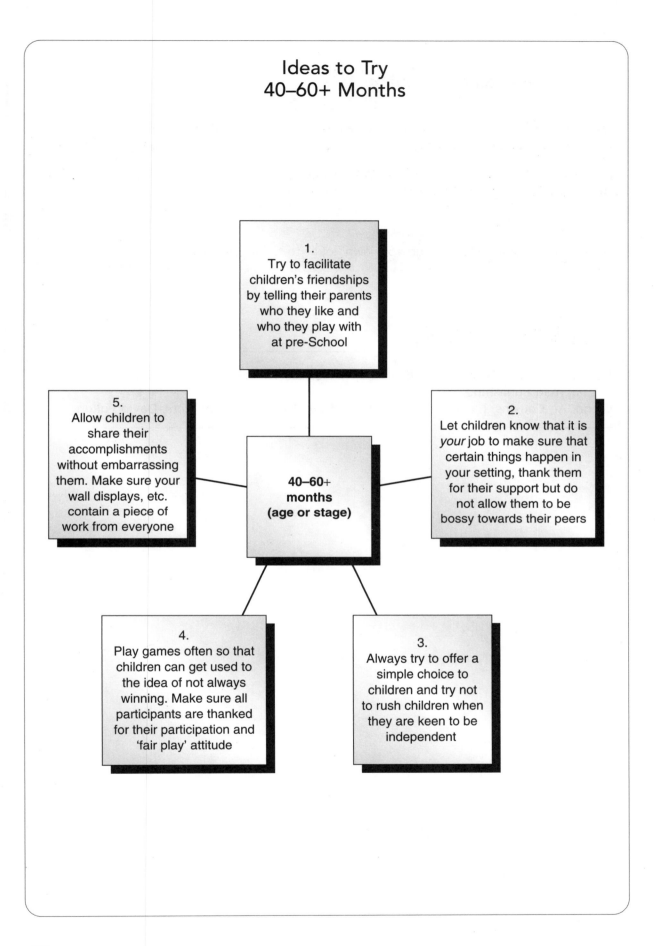

1.
Try to facilitate children's friendships by telling their parents who they like and who they play with at pre-School

5.
Allow children to share their accomplishments without embarrassing them. Make sure your wall displays, etc. contain a piece of work from everyone

40–60+ months (age or stage)

2.
Let children know that it is *your* job to make sure that certain things happen in your setting, thank them for their support but do not allow them to be bossy towards their peers

4.
Play games often so that children can get used to the idea of not always winning. Make sure all participants are thanked for their participation and 'fair play' attitude

3.
Always try to offer a simple choice to children and try not to rush children when they are keen to be independent

Hands-on activity

Using your own knowledge of child development and your experience of children's behaviour draw up your own diagrams of the types of behaviours that are usual in young children.

Use the blank templates on the CD-ROM to create your own diagrams (perhaps making them specific to the age/stage of the children you are working with).

Display them in your staff room.

As an additional activity write up your own 'ideas to try' (again sharing good practice).

Further reading

Dowling, M. (2005) *Young Children's Personal, Social and Emotional Development*. Paul Chapman Publishing.

Glenn, A., Cousins, J. and Helps, A. (2004) *Behaviour in the Early Years*. David Fulton.

CHAPTER THREE

A whole child approach

The aim of this chapter is to encourage practitioners to take a holistic view of the child.

It sets out:

- the holistic development of a child
- what this development looks like in practice
- actions to consider when you have concerns
- factors which may affect behaviour
- dealing with children's feelings

and includes:

- a Hands-on activity
- Further reading.

All early years practitioners are aware that children, like adults, have a wide and varied home life and experience different relationships. They are part of a family and a wider community as well as members of the setting community. That is why early years practitioners have always viewed children holistically. This approach is reflected in the Early Years Foundation Stage.

When considering the individual needs of children it is important for practitioners to think about what they already know about a child. This means thinking about what is happening to the child both inside and outside the setting.

The diagram on page 00 supports practitioners in understanding the type of needs that a child may have at any given time. Through understanding a child's needs practitioners will be able to:

- put a child's behaviour in context;

- understand why a child is behaving the way they are;

- work out how best they can support that child to move on.

Taking a Holistic View

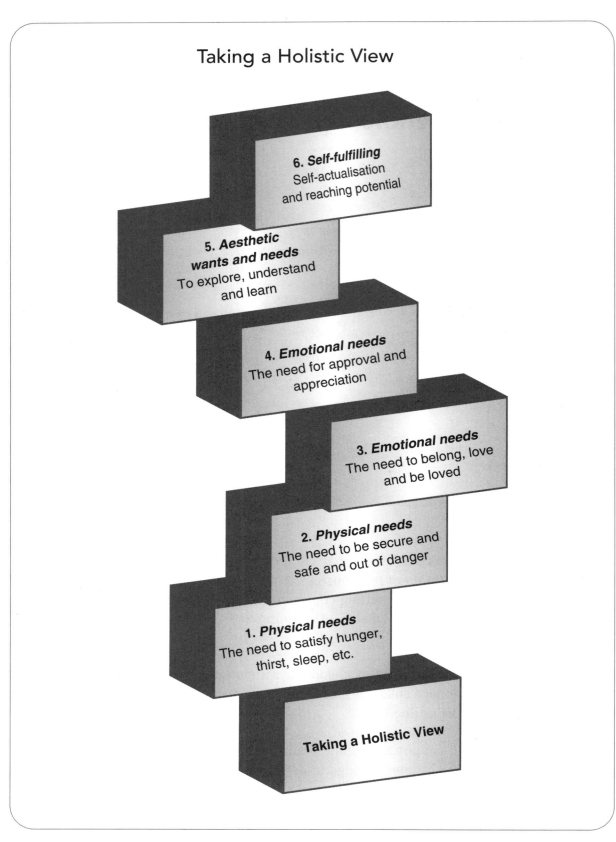

6. **Self-fulfilling**
Self-actualisation and reaching potential

5. **Aesthetic wants and needs**
To explore, understand and learn

4. **Emotional needs**
The need for approval and appreciation

3. **Emotional needs**
The need to belong, love and be loved

2. **Physical needs**
The need to be secure and safe and out of danger

1. **Physical needs**
The need to satisfy hunger, thirst, sleep, etc.

Taking a Holistic View

Based on Maslow's Hierarchy of Needs.
Source: Haynes, N. and Orrell, S. (1993) *Maslow in Psychology: An Introduction.* Harlow: Longman.

The diagram opposite shows pictorially the holistic development of a child. That is, it links all aspects of a child's life and shows how each aspect leads to another.

It demonstrates how young children need to have their basic needs met before they can move on to learn and discover, develop empathy, and live in harmony with their peers and the adults around them.

The role of early year's practitioners is to support children as they work their way through the stages of the diagram towards beginning to realise and reach their own potential.

Children who are near the top of the diagram are usually beginning to appreciate why they should behave well and will try to behave positively *most of the time*. They will be developing empathy and are beginning to understand the needs of others.

Different factors may impact upon children as events (most of which are out of the child's control) occur in their life. Reactions to these events and changing relationships may make some children move up and down through the stages. An obvious indicator of this is often seen in the way children behave.

This moving up and down through the stages also happens to adults and usually occurs as a reaction to an event or change of circumstance.

A strong foundation then must be laid in each step in order for the other levels to be securely built upon. If one level is insecure, then it will be difficult for a child to move on because all their needs are interrelated. The aim for practitioners is to support children to move onto stages 5 and 6 towards the top of the diagram:

Through careful observation and open communication with parents and carers practitioners should be able to identify when children are struggling. Practitioners and parents can then work together to support children back on track.

What the stages of the diagram may look like in practice: stages 1–4

1. 'The need to satisfy hunger, thirst, sleep, etc.'

 Case Study

Ahmed

▶ He has had a good night's sleep.

▶ He has had a drink and some cereal for breakfast.

▶ His mother dropped him off on time.

▶ His mother gave him a hug and said: 'See you later – I love you.'

Alfie

▶ He has been awake half the night because his baby brother was crying.

▶ He has had a biscuit for breakfast and is still hungry.

▶ His mother overslept so they had to rush to nursery.

▶ His mother was cross because he had been slow and left without saying goodbye.

How might both children behave?

The difference to the start of Ahmed's and Alfie's day can and probably would affect how they behave at nursery. Ahmed is ready for the day ahead and is probably keen to get on and be busy. Meanwhile, Alfie may be fretful, tired and possibly hungry.

What practitioners could do

Alfie could and should be given a cuddle and comforted. He could be given some breakfast before he sits down, perhaps for a one-on-one story with his key person. This would provide him with some nourishment and a rest. When he feels better he could join his friends. His key person should then, however, keep a close eye on him as he may be short-tempered and not at his best.

Alfie's Mum could be encouraged to get advice from her health visitor perhaps about sleep issues with her younger child as well as advice on how to set up routines within the home.

2. 'The need to be secure and safe and out of danger'

 Case Study

Hamida

Practitioners are worried about Hamida. Although she attends the setting happily she is very fretful when her mother leaves her. This is distressing both for Hamida and her mother. Throughout the day Hamida has to be taken away from the door where she sometimes sits waiting for her mother to return.

Hamida frequently upsets her friends by trying to take away the toys they are playing with. Practitioners have noticed that Hamida snatches toys from others then surprisingly doesn't even want to play with them herself. Instead she holds on tightly to the equipment or tries to puts it into her own special tray or lunch box.

Through a meeting with Hamida's parents practitioners have learned:

▶ Hamida's family are refugees who have fled their own country;

▶ the family have left all their belongings in their home country;

▶ some of their relatives have recently been deported back to their country of origin.

What practitioners could do

Hamida clearly isn't completely settled at the setting. She is insecure and worried that her mother won't return for her.

▶ A home visit could be arranged so that Hamida could see that her parents and her key person trust and respect each other.

▶ A new morning routine could be devised to ensure that Hamida is supported by both her mother and key person to feel more confident about being left. This could include using a visual timetable so that Hamida would know how the day was progressing and when her mother would be back.

▶ Hamida could be included in activities by all practitioners that would teach her how to play and share with her friends.

▶ One-on-one time could be arranged for Hamida and her key person.

▶ Hamida's mother could be encouraged to spend some time in the setting playing with Hamida and her friends.

▶ Hamida's family could be encouraged to use local toy and library services so that Hamida could get used to being around and playing with toys and equipment.

▶ The setting could send home some books and activities for Hamida to share with her family.

▶ Hamida and her family could be supported in meeting other members of the setting community by being invited to coffee mornings and other social events.

3. 'The need to belong, love and be loved'

Young children need to be part of the wider nursery community. They need to feel like they belong and that the adults around them feel affection for them and will care for them. In most cases this unquestionably happens but occasionally a child may go through an upset that affects their sense of belonging and being loved. This can happen to children without the adults around them realising and one of the most obvious results can be a change in the child's behaviour.

 Case Study

Peter

Peter is a confident child who has been at the setting for some time. He is well settled and liked by both the staff and his peers. Practitioners, however, have started to notice that Peter is becoming bad tempered and tearful. The slightest event seems to send him either into a rage or makes him cry.

Peter lives with his mother and often stays with his father at weekends.

Through a meeting with Peter's mother practitioners learned:

▶ Peter has been behaving in the same ways at home and his mother is also concerned;

▶ Peter has not stayed with his father for the previous three weeks as his grandmother was very ill and his father had returned to Scotland to help look after her.

What practitioners could do

Peter was obviously missing his father a lot and may even have been concerned about his grandmother. The practitioners hadn't been told about any of these changes in Peter's life and so hadn't made allowances for his feelings of insecurity and confusion.

▶ Peter's key person could encourage Peter's mother to bring in some photographs of Peter with his father as well as a photograph of his grandmother. Peter could share these with the staff and his friends.

▶ Peter could be encouraged to 'write a letter' and draw a picture for his father telling him how much he is looking forward to seeing him again.

▶ Peter could make a card and send it to his grandmother.

▶ Peter could have some extra one-on-one time with his key worker to talk through his feelings, sharing books, etc.

▶ Peter could be encouraged by staff to ask for their support if he is feeling cross or sad.

In this case simply by acknowledging Peter's feelings practitioners would go a long way to helping Peter to feel more like his own self.

4. 'The need for approval and appreciation'

A requirement of the EYFS in the Area of Learning and Development: Personal, Social and Emotional Development states:

> **Children must be provided with experiences and support which will help them to develop a positive sense of themselves and of others; social skills; and a positive disposition to learn. Providers must ensure support for children's emotional well-being to help them to know themselves and what they can do.**

(EYFS Practice Guidance, page 24)

Young children need the approval and appreciation of the adults around them and supporting a child to build their self-esteem is one of the most important aspects of early years practice.

The very foundations of all human beings' self-esteem are laid early in life. Children come to feel loved and accepted for who they are if the adults around them respond positively to their efforts and show them they value them.

Feeling good about yourself is the very core of self-esteem. If a child feels happy about how they are they will be confident and self-assured. This will become obvious by the way they learn and behave.

When children first leave the family home and make their way in a daycare or childminding setting they need to quickly develop a feeling of belonging to their new community. Practitioners become vitally important to a child's growing self-esteem as children become increasingly aware and sensitive about how others view them.

Children who display challenging behaviour may appear self-assured and confident but they rarely are. Instead, they more often have low self-esteem and are lacking in confidence. These children often don't feel good about themselves and are uncertain as to how they are viewed by the adults around them. Often these children find fitting in hard and often do not understand what is expected of them.

The guide below shows practitioners how to recognise how young children view themselves and their own self-esteem. Examples of 25 ways to build self-esteem can be found in the Skills Bank in Chapter 7.

Children and self-esteem

Children with *low* self-esteem often:

▶ display a strong need for reassurance, e.g. may constantly seek adult attention in a variety of ways which could include hitting, tantrums, etc.;

▶ appear to feel insecure, e.g. may need to know what is happening next and who they are going to be with, etc.;

▶ seem to feel safer when they take control, e.g. may appear bossy and demanding;

▶ seem to have no faith in their own capabilities, e.g. may destroy their own work or that of others;

▶ have problems learning, e.g. can be disruptive, refuse to listen or seem unwilling to cooperate;

▶ are reluctant to express their opinions, e.g. don't participate, are scathing about the contributions of others, etc.;

▶ find it hard to accept advice or comply with instructions;

▶ find it hard to make decisions, e.g. may flit from activity to activity;

▶ tend to over-react to not getting things 'right' or having to wait their turn;

▶ show little pride in their achievements;

▶ avoid trying new things;

▶ find getting along with other children difficult;

▶ have a low opinion of themselves, e.g. 'I can't do that', 'That's stupid', etc.

Children who have *high* self-esteem often:

▶ behave in an appropriate way, e.g. can judge in different situations what is the usual way to behave and do this without being asked (obviously not always!);

▶ learn fast and enjoy new experiences, e.g. like to listen and then try for themselves;

▶ are more willing to take risks when learning new things, e.g. can laugh at themselves when things go wrong and show perseverance;

▶ are more confident;

▶ are motivated to try;

▶ have consistent behaviour;

▶ make friends more easily;

▶ can act independently;

▶ show pride in their achievements;

▶ view other people with a positive interest, e.g. visitors, new staff and children, etc.;

▶ can accept suggestions and advice from both their peers and adults without giving up;

▶ develop a good sense of their own strengths and weaknesses even from a young age, e.g. are self-aware.

When practitioners are concerned about a child's behaviour – four actions to consider

1. Think about what you already know

A good place to begin if you have any concerns about a child is to gather information. Most practitioners know more than they think they do about individual children. Often it is only when we start to focus and really gather all the different pieces of information together that we begin to see the whole child.

▶ Consider what you already know about a particular child, their personality, likes, dislikes, etc.

▶ Talk to colleagues who may have a different view or perspective.

▶ Look at any written information such as your admissions form, previous reports, etc.

▶ Think about the child's strengths and areas which have improved or are developing well.

▶ Consider whether your concerns are new or whether you have always had them.

2. Think about what is happening in the child's life and family circumstances

There are many factors which can affect a child in the short term and for longer periods of time. These factors are mostly beyond your control but as practitioners you often have to deal with the consequences and effects on the child.

Some of the factors centre on physical needs such as lack of sleep, illness or poor living conditions. Some are connected to family circumstances such as bereavement or separation while others have their roots in change. Like adults many children find change quite difficult, whether it is moving into a new bedroom, a new house or having a new routine or carer.

While each child will react differently to a given set of circumstances, these factors can result in children displaying a whole range of needs. Practitioners may notice a change in a child's behaviour, concentration, attitude, emotional state or rate of progress. Use the diagram 'Taking a Holistic View' on page 20 to help you do this.

The diagram opposite illustrates some of the factors which *can* contribute to a child needing some extra support for a period of time.

3. Talk to parents

> **Parents are children's first and most enduring educators. When parents and practitioners work together in early years settings, the results have a positive impact on children's development and learning.**
>
> (EYFS Principles into Practice card 2.2)

Mutual respect, a valuing of diversity and effective communication are essential to forming good relationships with parents. These are particularly important when practitioners have to discuss more difficult issues or concerns about a child.

Any meeting should be regarded as a two-way exchange of information, with the possibility of both partners learning from each other. Discussions with parents can give practitioners insights into a child's personality, feelings or interests outside of the pre-school. Parents spend time with their child in varying situations – they can often inform practitioners about different sides of their child's personality.

It is very important that when you talk to a child's parents or carers about any concerns you may have that you are open-minded and non-judgemental. Discussions around any anxieties or concerns should be handled sensitively and in a way that will not cause alarm or appear as prying into their family life.

Careful thought and preparation should go into any meeting with practitioners, paying particular attention to the timing and place for any meeting. It is also essential to have a method of recording meetings with parents. Notes can be taken at the time and copies given to all involved. This ensures that practitioners and parents have a clear reminder of what was discussed and what was agreed at the meeting.

Some Social Factors Which Can Affect a Child's Progress or Behaviour

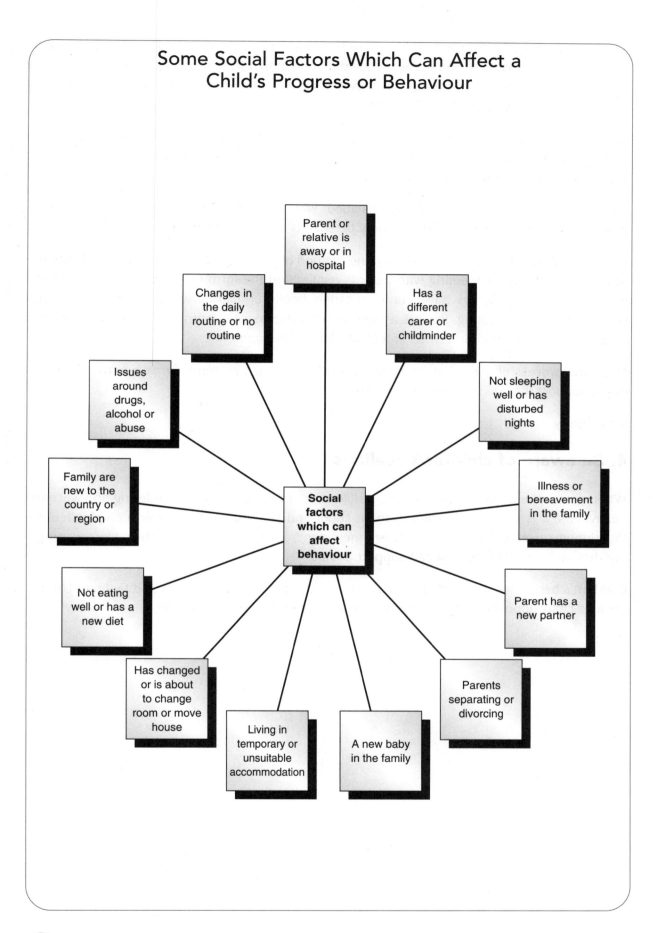

Parent or relative is away or in hospital

Changes in the daily routine or no routine

Has a different carer or childminder

Issues around drugs, alcohol or abuse

Not sleeping well or has disturbed nights

Family are new to the country or region

Social factors which can affect behaviour

Illness or bereavement in the family

Not eating well or has a new diet

Parent has a new partner

Has changed or is about to change room or move house

Living in temporary or unsuitable accommodation

A new baby in the family

Parents separating or divorcing

Sometimes a meeting can reveal that there have been changes in a child's life which parents may not have shared with you because they did not feel that they were important. While on the surface these might seem insignificant they can upset a child enough to make a difference to their behaviour, progress or development.

At other times there are changes which parents have not shared because they are very personal. It is very important therefore to make it clear *why* you are asking particular questions, i.e. that you are only interested in any factors which may be affecting their child.

You should also be very clear with parents about who you will be sharing any information with. Remember, some information should only be shared on a need-to-know basis.

It is very helpful if you already have a routine method of keeping in touch with parents. Many settings have systems for meeting with parents regularly in the form of either pastoral or general progress meetings. Others have communication books or diaries which go back and forth between home and setting. Parents as well as practitioners can contribute to observations and records which keep both informed of a child's latest developments.

Often the process of gathering information provides enough evidence for you to plan how you might support the child in their current situation.

And finally …

4. Be aware of children's feelings

When practitioners are considering the whole child, especially when considering any worrying behaviours, it is *always* necessary to think about and take into account how a child is feeling. Practitioners need to be able to reach into their own 'toolkit of skills' to find the necessary empathy they will need before they can support a child.

Children's behaviour – like adult's behaviour – is driven by their thoughts and feelings. Use the feelings chart opposite to help identify how some children may be feeling.

Dealing with Feelings

If children feel ...

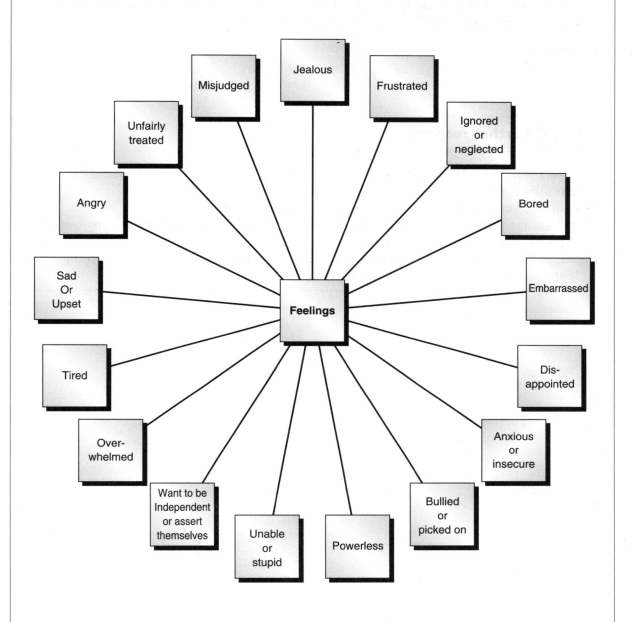

... it can lead to challenging behaviour

Hands-on activity

Using the diagram on page 31 for guidance draw up examples of when children may display the feelings mentioned, for example:

- *jealousy* – when a new baby arrives in the family, when one of their parents finds a new partner, when they hear others being praised or rewarded

- *bored* –

Further reading

Call, Nicole (2003) *The Thinking Child Resource Book*, The Early Years Series. Network Educational Press.

Donaldson, Margaret (1986) *Children's Minds*. HarperCollins.

Porter, Louise (2003) *Young Children's Behaviour: Practical Approaches for Caregivers and Teachers*. Paul Chapman Publishing.

Visser, Jo (2007) Supporting *Personal, Social and Emotional Development*, Everything Early Years How to … Series. Everything Early Years.

CHAPTER FOUR

The reflective setting

> The aim of this chapter is to support practitioners to reflect upon themselves, their practice and their environment and how it may affect the behaviour of the children in their setting.
>
> It outlines:
>
> ▶ the spiral of behaviour – a starting point for self-reflection
>
> ▶ team work
>
> ▶ how to write a behaviour policy
>
> ▶ improving aspects of your ethos, practice and environment
>
> ▶ audit and action plan
>
> and includes:
>
> ▶ a Hands-on activity
>
> ▶ Further reading.

There are many factors within a setting which can positively or negatively affect children's behaviour.

As well as looking at our own views, opinions and practice it is also important to look at our provision in the widest sense. There are some factors within a setting, for example, which can make it harder for children to behave well. It is worth, therefore, regularly reviewing the learning environment, activities and experiences that we are offering children to ensure that they also encourage and support better behaviour.

When we talk about behaviour the term 'whole-team approach' is often mentioned and this is because it is the *only* approach that will help build better behaviour in any setting. Every staff member will need to sign up to a particular way of thinking about children's behaviour and work consistently as a team in order for the approach to work successfully.

Creating a climate of collective responsibility and having a whole-team approach is not as simple as it sounds because working with children and their behaviours can be an emotive issue and one which can bring out strong and often differing views among staff teams. The following pages are designed to promote discussion and debate among staff teams and to help individuals think about their own views and practice. It will also help them to consider other factors within their setting which can affect children's behaviour.

Factors Within a Setting Which Positively Affect Behaviour

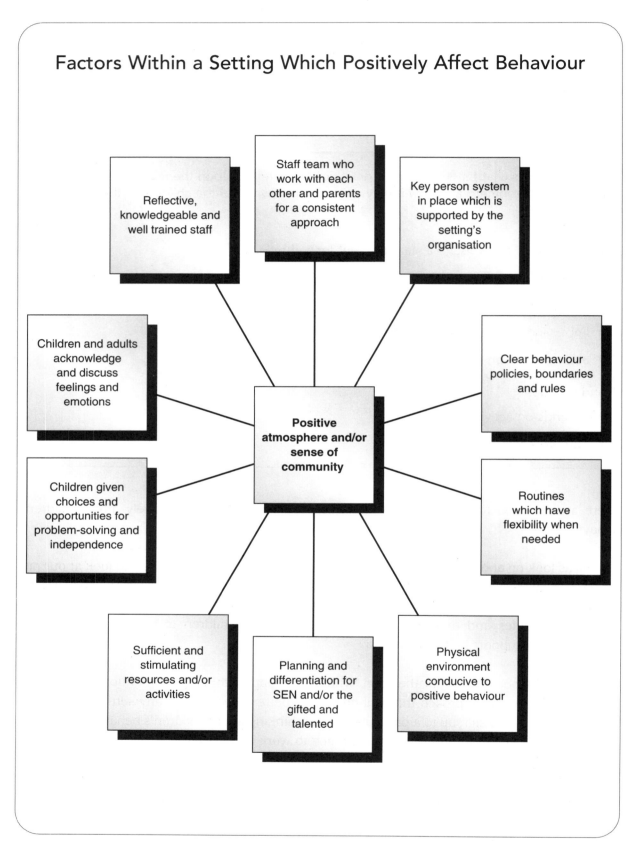

Reflective, knowledgeable and well trained staff

Reflection – looking at ourselves first

Often the process of reflection about children's behaviour begins too late, usually when situations have developed which have already become difficult or challenging. Sometimes it is a particular child or a particular incident that will spark off reflection about children's behaviour, how we can promote better behaviour and how we deal with inappropriate behaviour.

It is important that each person has time to reflect and that the issues are then discussed together as a team. In this way through reflection and debate a consensus can be reached about how your individual team will operate. As new situations arise, new members of staff join the team, new skills or knowledge are acquired and groups of children vary, this reflection and debate has to continue in order to adapt and remain relevant.

What affects how we interpret and/or respond to children's behaviour?

There are many factors which contribute to how we think about behaviour and how we deal with it as adults and as practitioners.

In the first instance we are all products of our background and upbringing. This can be affected by the views of our parents or carer, our culture, religion or education. It can be affected by our family makeup, experiences at school or work and our own values and beliefs.

Our interpretation and ability to respond to children's behaviour is also affected by our knowledge and self-awareness. Training, experience and good role models can inform our practice but without a level of self-awareness this is not always enough to help us deal with the children in our care or the situations in which we find ourselves.

Our own self-esteem, confidence and even how we are feeling physically, mentally or emotionally on any given day can affect how we behave ourselves and how we respond to the children. In the same way, these things affect the children themselves.

What Affects How We Interpret and/or Respond to Children's Behaviour?

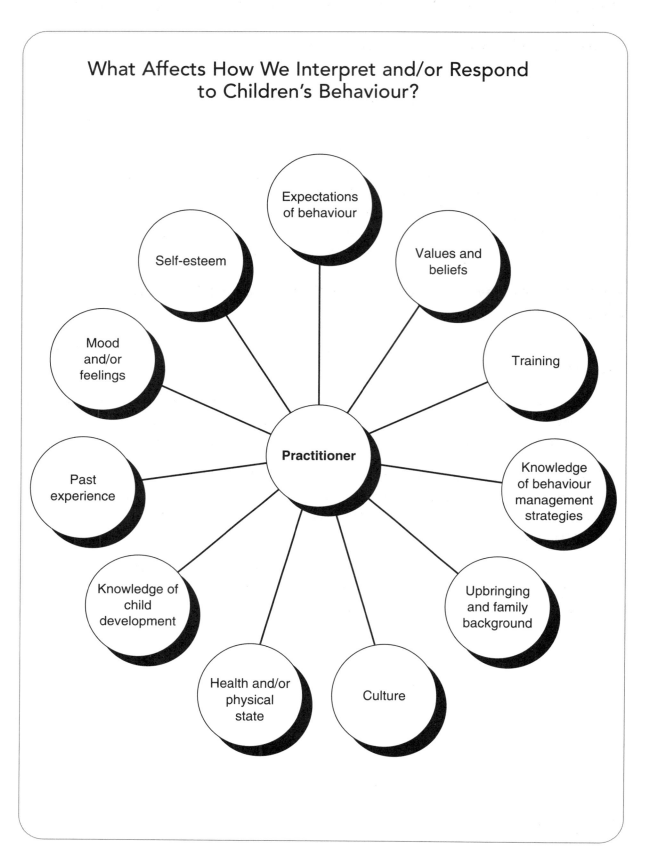

The spiral of behaviour

We can already see that our own thoughts and feelings feed into and help generate how we ourselves behave. So it is, too, for children.

Our response to a child's behaviour is extremely important as it can eventually, after repeated experience, determine the future behaviour of that child in what is sometimes called a spiral of behaviour.

Either a positive or negative spiral of behaviour can be created. Once a negative spiral is established it is very difficult, though not impossible, to turn it around, which is why it is so important to get things right before they go wrong.

The diagram opposite shows how this spiral is created.

▶ We can see that the child's thoughts and feelings lead to particular actions which begin the spiral.

▶ It is our interpretation of those actions which can change the spiral into either a negative or a positive direction.

▶ This is because our interpretation determines how *we* then behave.

▶ The interpretation also affects the language that we use.

▶ The language is particularly important because how we talk *about* and *to* a child shapes how we see the child but also how the child sees themselves.

▶ Our behaviour and language, in turn, have an effect on the child.

▶ The child will have a response which will affect how they feel generally but also how they feel about themselves and about us.

▶ These feelings will then affect how they might behave in the future.

When the experience of a child is a negative one and this pattern is repeated over and over again then behaviour can become fixed, almost like a habit.

We cannot always change the child's behaviour but we can change our own – that is where we need to start in order to change the direction of the spiral.

Spirals of Behaviour

Child's feelings trigger child's behaviour

Interpreted by the adult

 Child's experience creates feelings

Interpretation also generates adult feelings

Repetition of this cycle reinforces behaviour. A positive or negative spiral can be created depending on the responses

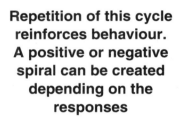

Child forms a perception of themselves

Adult responds to the child's behaviour as a result

Child forms a perception of the adult

Child responds to the adult's behaviour

 Adult forms a perception of the child

 Building Better Behaviour in the Early Years, SAGE © Chris Dukes and Maggie Smith, 2009

'It all depends on how you look at it'

Case Study

David is 3½ years old and attends the small local nursery for three mornings each week. There are three members of staff in the toddler room: Angela, Beverley, who is David's key person and Caroline.

Throughout the day David repeatedly throws things up into the air or over his shoulder. This happens even more at tidy-up time and staff are finding it very disruptive, particularly as other children are starting to copy.

Below are the ways the three different members of staff:

 - interpret what the child has done;
 - how it makes the staff member feel;
 - how they subsequently deal with the behaviour;
 - the consequences for the child.

Staff member – Angela

David knows that he is not supposed to throw things around the pre-school setting but carries on being deliberately disruptive. He laughs and encourages the other children to join in. Angela feels angry because she feels that David is being deliberately naughty and disobeying her, even though he knows he shouldn't.

David is told not to do this and given two minutes' time out to think about what he is doing wrong. His behaviour is reported to his mother at the end of the morning.

Angela watches David closely for the rest of the week and warns colleagues about his behaviour.

David is upset during time out and feels unhappy. He also gets into trouble with his mother at the end of the morning. He feels angry that the staff always seem to be telling him to stop what he is doing.

Staff member – Beverley

David is very attention-seeking and seems to be looking at the adults in the room as he throws things, as if he wants them to notice him. His behaviour is worse at tidy-up time because all the adults are busy and the other children are moving around a lot. He doesn't like helping to tidy anyway.

Beverley feels deskilled because she is David's key person but he doesn't seem to take any notice of her. Other members of staff are making comments about this which makes her feel worse.

David is told not to throw things and, unless the throwing is dangerous, Beverley ignores him as far as possible when he does it. As David's key person she also makes a point of asking David to tidy up with her as he has to learn to do this.

David feels that Beverley doesn't like him because she doesn't talk to him or play with him very much. He tries to get everyone else's attention by shouting when he throws things.

Staff member – Caroline

David is fascinated by what happens when you throw something up in the air. This is probably part of a schema but the difficulty is caused when he throws inappropriate things at inappropriate times. He laughs and looks around for other children and adults to show them what he can do.

Caroline feels confident that she can to do something positive to change David's behaviour to prevent him from being labelled as being naughty.

David is told that he should not throw random things around, especially at tidy-up time. A small indoor space and a larger outdoor space are made where a selection of beanbags, balls, hoops and soft toys are provided. David is included in a small group of children who are shown a variety of activities which involve throwing and catching.

David still has to be reminded about helping to tidy up and when he can and can't throw things but is really enjoying the activities. He has shown the other children and Caroline how high and how far he can throw the beanbags. His catching skills are also improving.

Hands-on activity

1. Discuss this case study with colleagues.
2. Which member of staff do you identify with most?
3. Would a critical friend have been useful to Angela and Beverley?
4. Think of similar situations you may have encountered and how you might handle them differently.

A note about schemas

Most parents and practitioners will have seen children and toddlers repeating the same actions over and over again, or repeatedly playing the same game in the same way over and over. When a child does this we have an insight into how they are thinking and learning.

Schemas can manifest themselves in many ways and often some of these ways seem inappropriate and can be disruptive. The child's actions are therefore misinterpreted and they could be labelled as displaying 'bad behaviour'.

If practitioners recognise a schema for what it is, however – a way of children learning and developing their knowledge – children can be shown how to direct their actions into more appropriate forms.

Look at 'Let's Talk About … Schemas' in Chapter 7 on page 93.

Team work

Unfortunately despite the fact that behaviour should be viewed very much as a **collective responsibility** in many settings certain members of staff will be looked upon as being more responsible for behaviour issues than others.

Sometimes this person is the named practitioner referred to in the EYFS, sometimes the special needs or inclusion coordinator and sometimes a member of staff who just seems most successful at dealing with more challenging children.

The EYFS states quite clearly that there should be a named practitioner who should be responsible for behaviour management issues. It goes on to say that this person should be supported in acquiring skills to provide guidance to other staff members and to access expert advice. So while the **'named practitioner'** may take the lead in matters of behaviour within the setting, they are not solely responsible for it.

The **key person** is also central to current thinking and the benefits of having this system are many. However, the while the key person may be the one who develops a close and secure attachment to an individual child, again they should not be regarded as the only person who can deal with that child's behaviour should the need arise. This is particularly important to remember when working with children with challenging behaviour which can be extremely difficult and lonely if a practitioner is left unsupported by others in the team.

Working as a team is never as easy as it sounds but in terms of behaviour it is crucial. It is something which needs to be worked upon and constantly reviewed and re-evaluated. This is not easy when days are busy and time is short.

Below are some simple suggestions for keeping behaviour on the staff team agenda.

Ten suggestions for keeping behaviour on the staff team agenda

1. Review your behaviour policy

Although this should be carried out annually many settings' behaviour policies remain unchanged for many years because the review is brief or it is a matter of merely rubberstamping the existing policy. The importance of having an up-to-date policy is explained later in this chapter.

2. Carry out an audit of behaviour training courses your team has attended

This is an area which is often overlooked when there are so many other pressures on time – a little investment, however, can make a real difference. Training is often provided by local authorities via their advisory teams or it can be accessed through private organisations. Wherever possible it is best for whole staff teams to attend behaviour training together. Where this is not possible individuals should try to cascade what they have learnt.

3. Sometimes it is difficult to know where to start a discussion about behaviour

The audit later in the chapter can help by focusing staff on how they feel about behaviour themselves and how they see it in the setting.

4. Have a 'behaviour slot' at each team meeting

This is a perfect opportunity to discuss issues that have arisen during the week. If the atmosphere is supportive practitioners can be encouraged to take turns or be spontaneous and talk about an event or a behaviour that they found challenging or would like advice about from colleagues.

5. Make sure you 'debrief' after handling any particularly difficult behaviour

It can be exhausting physically, mentally and emotionally dealing with difficult behaviour. Without some sort of debriefing, staff can go home with a range of different feelings about themselves and individual children. It is healthy to share these with someone else and to make sure that any outstanding issues are dealt with or plans are made to deal with them so that no one feels isolated or upset.

6. Have a 'critical friend'

The idea of a critical friend is to have someone whom you trust and respect who can help you to think about your own behaviour and practice. Often we are too close to situations to analyse what is going on, especially if emotions are running high.

Our critical friend can offer suggestions and ask questions to help us focus on how we handled a situation, our body language, facial expressions, tone of voice or strategies used.

7. Establish a way of sharing successful strategies for individual children with other members of staff

When you find that a particular strategy works with an individual child, it is very helpful to tell other staff members about it. This not only gives consistency but can help widen the repertoire of everyone on your team. Some strategies only work for a short time and then new ones have to be employed so it is important that everyone is up to speed with the latest developments.

A notebook, jottings on a behaviour plan or memos on a staff noticeboard (if it is in a private area) are all good ways of doing this.

8. Have a strategy of the week

All practitioners use a range of strategies to deal with behaviour. Sometimes, however, these are quite limited and ideas we picked up or tried but never really established as part of our everyday practice are forgotten. It can be helpful to remind ourselves of a strategy that others use but that we don't or vice versa. This doesn't mean that it is the only strategy we use all week but it can help us to try out and focus on something different!

9. Have a 'behaviour' of the week

This means that for any particular week practitioners would try to look out for or even note down whenever a particular behaviour occurs – biting, for example. Staff might note down who is biting, who is being bitten, when, where, how it is being dealt with, strategies used, etc. This can then be discussed to see if there is consistency among staff, if there is any pattern to what happens, etc. In this way discussion is encouraged and a whole-team approach can be developed.

10. Involve parents

How to encourage 'good' behaviour and how to manage behaviour which is inappropriate is not just an issue for practitioners. Many parents find it very difficult to know what to do and often feel very inadequate. Equally, they have the best knowledge about their individual child and this can be enormously helpful when difficulties occur.

Ways of working with parents include the following:

▶ Make sure that you maintain dialogue with parents and that they are fully aware of your behaviour policy.

▶ Maintain communication in as many ways you can – e-mail, text, tapes as well as letters and phone calls.

▶ Use setting–home diaries for children who may need extra support, but remember to be positive.

▶ Think about hosting parent support groups or parenting classes at your setting which can offer help and support to parents and carers.

▶ Help parents to have some insight into their child's behaviour by sharing information such as the 'Let's Talk About …' leaflets and signpost them to other sources of advice.

A clear behaviour policy

Why behaviour policies matter

It is essential for every setting to have its own unique behaviour policy. It may be easier to adopt a ready-made policy from the many that are already in existence but it will never be as meaningful as one which has been agreed by a staff team. Ready-made policies should be regarded as templates which give a starting point for discussion and an opportunity to explore what matters to individuals within a team. In this way a tailor-made policy is created which is agreed by everyone and meets the needs of your own particular setting. Such a policy is more likely to be used and have value when everyone on the team has had some input and feels a degree of ownership. As with other policies it should be reviewed regularly and this is particularly important if there are changes in staff.

What a behaviour policy should contain

▶ A **rationale** which reflects the **ethos** and **commitment** of your setting and staff.

▶ **How** you will **implement** the behaviour policy – by having:

- a written policy;

- procedures and guidelines for managing behaviour;

- staff and volunteers' induction;

- a method of sharing policy with parents;

- a designated member of staff with responsibility for behaviour issues;

- access to behaviour management training;

- knowledge of national guidelines on physical intervention;

- methods of reporting incidents to parents;

- clearly defined responses to unacceptable behaviour;

- appropriate use of staff to support the development of children's relationships and social skills;

- clear and high expectations of behaviour.

▶ An outline of your **practice** will help promote positive behaviour – by:

- the organisation of the environment;

- the provision of relevant resources and activities;

- a consistent and positive approach;

- responses appropriate to children's age and stage of development;

- staff modelling good behaviour in their own interactions;

- the encouragement of awareness of routines and procedures;

- clear boundaries and expectations;

- observation and recording of significant behaviour;

- dealing immediately with negative behaviour;

- identifying and promoting successful strategies.

▶ **Methods** of **promoting** positive behaviour – which could include:

- providing play and learning experiences which explore and encourage positive behaviour such as circle time, puppets and persona dolls, stories and role play;

- enabling children to experience success so supporting and building self-esteem;

- encouraging and developing children's ability to describe and express their feelings;

- supporting children to resolve disputes and conflict;

- modelling appropriate language and behaviour at all times;

- establishing routines and facilitating activities which encourage sharing, turn taking and cooperation.

- promoting a caring attitude to their environment and others by helping and sharing responsibilities such as tidying up and preparing snack time;

- using 'labelled' praise to reward specific actions or behaviour;

- making explicit what is acceptable behaviour and discussing this with children;

- helping children understand the effects and consequences of their behaviour;

- demonstrating that the child is still liked and valued even if his/her behaviour is unacceptable;

- involving children and parents in establishing 'golden rules' for behaviour.

Routines

▶ Have established routines but with some flexibility built in. These provide a sense of safety and reassurance for most children.

▶ Have an element of predictability so that children know what is happening and what to expect from each session.

▶ Consider using a *visual timetable* for the group.

▶ Make sure that you talk about and prepare children for changes in the routine such as special visitors, trips or new activities.

▶ Give advance warning of when an activity is about to change or stop.

▶ A five-, two- and then one-minute warning can be very helpful in encouraging children to finish what they are doing.

▶ Allow for those children who may want to continue later by helping them to put away their model or painting etc. in a safe place so that they can return to it later.

▶ Establish turn-taking systems for activities or toys which are in high demand such as bikes!

▶ Use sand timers, kitchen timers, wrist bands, badges, names on a chalk board or Velcro board, or have a limited number of chairs or aprons to show when an activity is 'full'.

▶ Be prepared to 'go with the flow' occasionally!

A well planned physical environment

▶ Audit your room by getting down to a child's level and seeing it as they do.

▶ Have some display boards at a child's eye level. Encourage them to display their own work.

▶ When planning your room position furniture and activities carefully.

▶ Ensure that there are no 'run through' routes.

▶ Have designated areas outside or inside and particular spaces where running about is allowed.

▶ Define activity spaces using shelving and furniture.

▶ Set up some areas that are shielded from pathways, exits, etc. This stops 'walk/run through' which also often leads to knock over!! This can be particularly important for construction or small-world type activities.

▶ Have areas that are stimulating, varied and well set up. They should look inviting and staff and children should be encouraged to have pride in their setting.

▶ Have a quiet area where children can go to relax, calm down or just be by themselves for a while. This may be an area with a low screen around it or even a tent or den to feel safe and secure inside.

▶ Make sure that each child has a small piece of personal space to store their belongings, models or pictures as well as a coat peg.

▶ Make sure that you have thought about and planned for children with a variety of needs.

Planning and differentiation

▶ Make sure there are resources and materials to allow children to access the same activity at different levels.

▶ Anticipate and plan for the children who may need support at different activities, either to help them access an activity or to extend them.

▶ Include children's individual plans such as individual education plans or behaviour support plans into the whole-group planning.

▶ Make sure that children's individual interests and strengths are built into your plans.

Activities and resources

▶ Ensure that there are sufficient resources to allow children to share effectively or take turns but that there is not an overabundance of materials taking up all available space.

▶ Set up activities in a way that minimises overcrowding. Have clear ways of showing when an area is 'full' or how many children should be at an activity.

▶ Children need to see that things are fair. Have some good systems in place so that some children are not left to dominate activities while others are always left to wait.

▶ Make sure that you have thought about and planned for children with a variety of needs and learning styles.

▶ Provide resources that will encourage collaborative play.

Independence, choice and problem solving

▶ Allow for children to be independent and to make choices.

▶ Encourage them to select resources; help them to 'plan and do' and to decide what they would like to use.

▶ Ensure that equipment is stored at a level which is easily accessible and is clearly labelled.

▶ Teach children to leave resources and play areas ready for the next person. Unless they are saving for later, expect children to 'complete the circle of activity'. Plan, do and tidy away.

▶ Encourage children to talk about difficulties or problems. Try not to offer solutions immediately but ask them what they think they could do to resolve the situation.

Acknowledge and discuss feelings and emotions

▶ Help children to give their own feelings a name or label.

▶ Have illustrations and play games which can help children recognise emotions in others.

▶ Talk about how *you* are feeling and why.

▶ A useful phrase when discussing children's behaviour with them is 'When you ... I feel ...'

▶ Use stories, puppets and persona dolls to help talk about feelings and emotions.

▶ Let children know that it is OK to feel angry or sad and help them to have a way of letting you know how they are feeling.

▶ Have regular circle time to talk together.

Audit
Does Our Setting Encourage Positive Behaviour?

Area to be considered Do you have …	Yes	No	Could be improved
A reflective and knowledgeable staff team			
Access to training on behaviour issues			
A staff team who work with each other for a consistent approach			
A staff team who work with parents for a consistent approach			
A key person system in place which is supported by the setting's organisation			
A clear behaviour policy			
Clear boundaries and rules			
Routines which have flexibility when needed			
A physical environment conducive to positive behaviour			
Planning and differentiation for SEN			
Planning and differentiation for the gifted and talented			
Sufficient and stimulating resources for a range of needs and abilities			
Sufficient and stimulating activities for a range of needs and abilities			
Opportunities for children to make choices and experience independence			
Opportunities for problem-solving			
Children and adults who acknowledge and discuss feelings and emotions			

Action Plan

Identified need (e.g. training, resources)	Action and by whom (e.g. organise, order)	When	Cost	Completed
Whole team				
Individual team members				

Hands-on activity

1. Look at the diagram 'Factors within a setting which positively affect behaviour' on page 34. and think about how each of the factors shown might have affected your behaviour and response to a child in the past.

2. Is there anything you could learn from this?

3. How would this knowledge change your practice?

Further reading

Paige-Smith, Alice and Craft, Anna (2006) *Reflective Practice in the Early Years*. Open University Press.

CHAPTER FIVE

A strategy bank

The aim of this chapter is to provide practitioners with 25 key strategies to incorporate into their everyday practice. These strategies will foster and encourage better behaviour in your setting.

It outlines:

▶ everyday strategies

▶ listening and talking to children

▶ adults supporting both children and each other

▶ examples of the strategies in practice

and includes:

▶ a Hands-on activity

▶ Further reading.

The strategies explained

Practitioners need to feel confident that they can deal with a variety of events and situations in a calm professional way. By building up your own strategy bank you will begin to develop confidence in your practice.

Outlined below is a range of well tried and tested behaviour strategies that many practitioners already use to help create a positive pre-school.

25 Golden Behaviour Strategies
for Practitioners and Parents

Everyday strategies

1. Try to offer choices
2. Practise planned ignoring
3. Use distraction
4. Remove a child(ren) from a potential situation
5. Be a facilitator

Listening and talking

6. Acknowledge children's feelings
7. Make face-to-face contact
8. Keep language simple
9. Discuss difficult behaviour later
10. De-personalise situations that need to be talked about
11. Have clear expectations and share these with the children
12. Avoid empty praise
13. Use specific praise statements
14. Offer choice statements

Adults supporting both children and each other

15. Adults as positive role models
16. Model the desired behaviour
17. Show a united front and support each other
18. Consistency
19. Being seen to be fair
20. An ounce of prevention – give positive attention before an incident occurs
21. Work in partnership with parents
22. Share the challenge of difficult behaviour
23. Try not to bargain with a child
24. Make time to reflect after a difficult episode
25. Acknowledge considerate behaviour with a simple 'thank you'

Everyday strategies

Try to offer choices

Always try to give children choices and give them a way out of a difficult situation. This is especially helpful on those occasions when a situation has escalated quickly and children seem to have backed themselves into a corner where they don't want to back down.

Example

Sarah refused to come and sit on the carpet for story time. Her key person, Mary, calmly said to Sarah 'Ok, Sarah, where would you like to sit? On this little chair by me or on the floor on the red cushion?'

Sarah chose to sit on the red cushion.

The situation was resolved quickly and Sarah saved face as she was able to make a choice.

Practise planned ignoring

Sometimes it is best to 'planned ignore'. This often defuses a situation and gives the child time to make a 'good decision'.

This strategy can be used when the child or children or equipment is not likely to come to any harm.

Example

During an outside activity Reuben was seen to be in the corner pushing the Duplo off a workbench onto the ground. Farhana, his key person, was busy with the other children making kites. Farhana continued with the activity ignoring Reuben. When the children had made their kites Farhana said: 'Let's all go into the big garden to run with our kites.' On hearing this Reuben rejoined the group. Farhana let Reuben use the spare kite she had made. The children all enjoyed running in the wind.

After the activity Farhana took Reuben's hand and while still chatting about the activity started picking up the Duplo pieces. She said, 'Can you help me please, Reuben,' and together they cleared up the duplo.

Remember: Children will not tend to repeat behaviour that receives no response.

Use distraction

To use distraction practitioners need to have a good overview of what is happening in the room. The layout of a room should always be considered carefully.

This strategy is particularly useful in supporting children to avoid confrontation with their peers and to help them to share and play together.

Example

Tom and another child both wanted to use the same doll and buggy. Reena, a practitioner, could see that the other child was engrossed in her imaginative play and the buggy was an integral part of her activity.

On seeing what was about to happen Reena said in an excited voice, 'Oh look, Tom, the garage is free now. If you hurry over here you can have your turn and we can play together.'

Alternatively Reena could have also said to Tom: 'Oh, Tom, I really need you to help me. Can you come over here please.'

When the other child had finished with the doll and buggy Reena offered it to Tom and said: 'I think you waited really well for your turn, Tom. Would you like the doll and buggy now?'

Remove a child(ren) from a potential situation

Sometimes a whole situation can be avoided by simply removing a child(ren) from a potential upset.

Example

While on a nursery trip to the zoo Rhia, a key person, was leading a small group. It was almost lunchtime and the children were going to have a picnic. Rhia noticed that there was an ice cream vendor further down the path which none of the children had yet noticed. To avoid any situation arising Rhia simply led her group down a different path avoiding the potential conflict.

Be a facilitator (and not a referee!)

Children need to be encouraged and supported to resolve conflicts and disagreements themselves. This doesn't always lead to a decision that suits all parties but it is an important part of the learning process. Remember to remain neutral in children's disputes and try not to take sides.

Example

In the home corner Arniv and Hattie are involved in a tussle over a teapot. Both children are pulling at the equipment. Sonia, a practitioner, tries to reason with the pair to find out who had the teapot first. Neither child can agree on how to share the teapot. Sonia says: 'Well, I am sorry, but I can see you are not willing to share at the moment so I will take the teapot away so you can both get on with your game.'

Neither child was happy at the result. A few minutes later they both approached Sonia and asked if they could share the teapot. Sonia said that would be lovely and could she please have a cup of tea.

Listening and talking

Try to acknowledge children's feelings

When a child is cross or angry or sad always try to acknowledge how they are feeling. This shows that you are sympathetic and 'tuned in' to a child. This acknowledgement often goes a long way to calming a child down.

Example

Following an upset Omas got very cross with one of the practitioners; he yelled and screamed and tried to hit her. Jess, his key person, went over to help. She held Omas gently and said, 'I can see that you are very angry right now.'

This acknowledgement helped Omas calm down and the practitioners manage to resolve the situation with him.

Note that the key person did not agree with Omas's actions but she did recognise his emotions.

In this case the key person, Jess, later that morning worked one-on-one with Omas to talk through the situation and helped Omas think about different solutions.

Make face-to-face contact

When talking to a child and especially when checking or correcting a child's behaviour, bend down and get face-to-face contact before speaking. (Note that this does not necessarily mean direct eye contact.)

Several things are achieved when you take the time to do this:

▶ Adults are not shouting over the room at children so you are being a good role model.

▶ You are giving the child individual attention, which is possibly what he/she needs at that moment in time.

▶ You are able to ensure the child has heard and understands what you are saying. This avoids misunderstandings occurring.

First say the child's name, then bend in front of them and speak in a calm and controlled way.

Never ever glare at, shout at, or scare a child. If another member of staff does this find the time later to discuss it with them or inform your line manager about your unease at how some staff members talk to children.

Keep language simple

When issuing an instruction or explaining something to a child, try to keep your language as simple as possible. If in doubt 'check out' what you have said to the child to make sure he/she understands. If you think the child hasn't understood rephrase what you have said.

Example

While outside Rosie became upset. She wanted to have a turn with the children's favourite red pushbike. A practitioner said to Rosie, 'I will put your name on the list so you can have your turn on the bike.' Rosie then tried to push another child off the bike saying, 'It's my turn – she says so.'

Rosie has misunderstood what has been said to her.

A possible solution

The practitioner could have helped Rosie put her name on the waiting list for a bike. She could have told Rosie who was before her on the list. She could have 'checked out' Rosie's understanding of the situation by asking Rosie to recap whose turn is before hers.

Discuss difficult behaviour later

When children are upset, angry or distressed remember to ***acknowledge the feeling***. If this is done it is often best not to probe and over-analyse the behaviour that has just happened. Instead, encourage the children to be reflective about it later.

Once a child is cross or upset they often feel '**flooded**' with an emotion. While flooded any chance of a reasonable discussion with the child is limited. Once a child calms down and is again '**balanced**' the situation can then be talked through.

This can also be true of practitioners.

Being 'Emotionally Flooded'

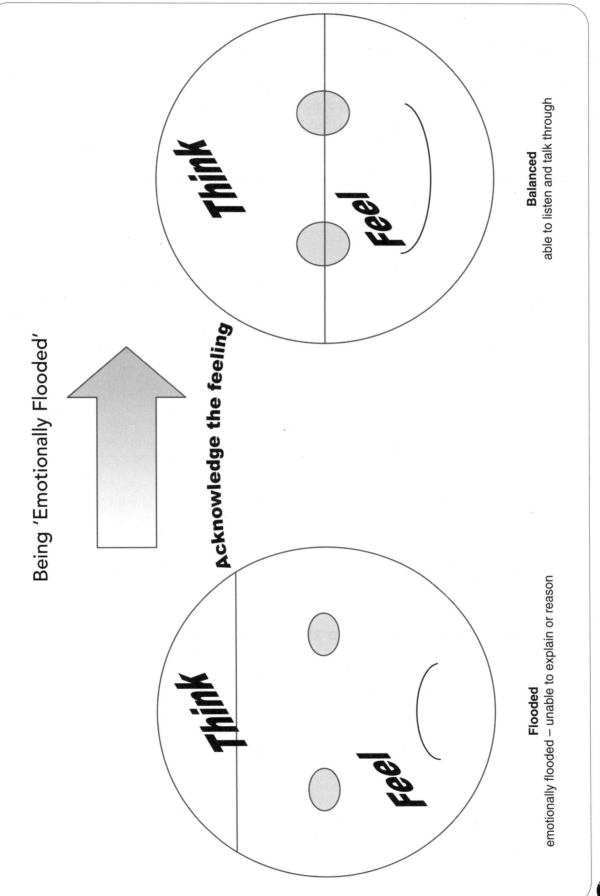

acknowledge the feeling

Flooded
emotionally flooded – unable to explain or reason

Balanced
able to listen and talk through

Building Better Behaviour in the Early Years, SAGE © Chris Dukes and Maggie Smith, 2009

See the diagram above for a pictorial view of how it feels to be 'flooded' and 'balanced'.

De-personalise situations that need to be talked about

Avoid talking about particular instances and specific children in the nursery. Instead talk about the issues that may have been raised by using puppets, persona dolls, story books, role play and circle time. Use these times to create scenarios. This de-personalises situations and helps children to see how their actions both affect and appear to others.

Encourage children to think about issues from the viewpoint of others.

(EYFS Practice Guidance, page 36)

Example

While in the garden with the children, Rose, a practitioner, saw an incident. Liam approached a small group of boys who were engrossed in an imaginative play activity. He stood on the sidelines for a while watching then started to join in the play. Tom, one of the other children, said to him: 'Oh not you, we don't want you to play with us. Go away.' Liam immediately left the scene and helped Rose set up a picinic in the garden for all the children to enjoy.

Later that morning Rose used the setting's persona dolls Tim and Molly to replay the scene, looking at the scenario from different perspectives. The children enthusiastically offered their ideas and comments including those involved in the incident. The session finished with Tom saying, 'Sometimes people can be mean to others when they don't really mean to be.' Rose acknowledged that, yes, sometimes this was the case and asked the children for possible solutions.

The children all agreed that if a child wanted to play with others he/she should be able to as they were all friends together.

Of course the children would need reminding of their decision by practitioners but the situation had been discussed without naming names and getting personal and more importantly the children had found their own solutions.

Have clear expectations and share these with the children

Do not feel you have to give an explanation for everything, i.e. keep things simple. That way your expectations are clear. Clear expectations are much more likely to be met.

> **Example**
>
> Leah, a practitioner, wanted the children to put their coats on to go out to play. She said, 'Right, everybody, listen. I want you all to go into the corridor and get your coats and put them on. Remember to fasten them because it is a very cold day today and I don't want anyone catching a cold.'
>
> All she had to say was 'Please put your coats on' while role modelling putting her own coat on.
>
> Similarly Leah later said, 'I need you all to sit down, with your legs crossed, here on the carpet because we are all going to listen to the story of The Three Bears.' All she had to say was, 'Please come here and sit down,' while moving over to the story area herself.

Avoid empty praise

Everyone has been on the receiving end of 'good boy', 'good girl' type praise. If it is said often enough it ends up having little meaning to those on the receiving end.

When praising children try to be more specific, e.g. 'You are so good at sharing' *or* 'I am really impressed by how you shared the book with Mary' *or* 'You are such a hard-working group of children you have tidied up brilliantly today.'

Remember, some children are embarrassed by 'over the top' praise and sometimes it is sufficient to give a smile or a nod of even a thumbs up sign. This means you can praise children quietly and discretely or even when standing away from them. (See '25 Ways to Say Well Done' on page 91.)

Sometimes sincere interest can be more effective and meaningful than praise. Try to show a genuine interest in what the children are doing and saying. If it is heartfelt the children will appreciate it more than empty praise statements.

Use specific praise statements

By using praise statements children can be encouraged to behave in a positive way. This is an effective strategy as adults can get the children to do what is required without actually telling the children to do it! And the children are happy to do something as they haven't been told specifically to do it.

Children cooperate because they are reminded something needs to be done and also because they want to please their parent or practitioner.

Say, 'It would be great if you could finish off that puzzle before lunchtime' instead of, 'I want that puzzle finished and put away right now.'

Or, 'It's brilliant the way you are sitting quietly on the mat' instead of, 'Can you all sit quietly.'

Or, 'It's great the way you all put your coats on when it is time to go outside to play' instead of, 'Before we go outside I want to see everyone with their coat on.'

> *A note of caution regarding praise*
>
> **Children need to know that they are cared for and valued because of who they are and not just because they have pleased an adult or achieved a goal.**

Offer choice statements

Choice statements encourage and teach children how to make good choices regarding their behaviour. They help to show children that they always have a choice over the way they behave and what they do, e.g. they *can* wait their turn, or they *can* play at another activity, etc.

Choice statements also help children practise their decision-making skills as well as teaching them to become responsible for their own behaviour.

A choice statement by a practitioner provides children with the necessary prompt to think about their behaviour and how it affects others. It also reminds children that they have the choice to 'do the right thing'.

The EYFS Practice Guidence recognises this as an important area of learning for young children when it says children need to be supported to:

▶ Value and contribute to own well-being and self control …

▶ Consider the consequences of their words and actions for themselves and others.

(Early Learning Goals 40–60+ months, pages 33 and 36)

Example

Leo was playing in the sand tray with three other children. He was irritating the other children by leaning over and knocking down their sandcastles. Peter, a practitioner, said to Leo: 'Play nicely in the sand or come away, it's *your* choice.' Leo changed his behaviour as he was enjoying playing in the sand with his friends. Peter smiled at Leo and gave him a thumbs up sign of approval at his good decision.

Adults supporting children and each other

Adults as positive role models

Children learn from those adults around them, therefore practitioners are best placed to show children what positive behaviours look like. Adults who are courteous towards each other and who never raise their voice provide excellent role models for young children. Setting staff need to be aware of their own code of conduct within the setting. It is the responsibility of the manager to ensure that all setting staff maintain the highest standards of personal behaviour while at work.

Remember, young children learn through observation and doing and they are observing practitioners at work all day.

Model the desired behaviour

Show the child what to do as well as saying it.

Example

During tidy-up time Tina, the key person, would always struggle to get Luke to participate and help. Tina asked Luke to help her tidy away a jigsaw, but she finished off most of the jigsaw, picking the pieces up from the floor herself while Luke watched her. Tina managed to get Luke to put the last two pieces of puzzle in by pretending she didn't know where they went. Tina then praised Luke's efforts and thanked him for his help. Luke was left with a feeling of pride and a sense of achievement.

Remember: Children will repeat behaviour that receives a positive response.

Show a united front and support each other

Staff should work as a team backing each other up. This lets children know that what every member of staff says matters. Personal conflicts with individual children should always be avoided and staff need to support each other to ensure this does not happen.

Example

Bilal, a practitioner, was carrying out a very messy creative activity with those children who wanted to participate. She had prepared the children beforehand and had outlined that those children who wanted to participate would need to wait their turn and wear an apron.

Haroon waited patiently for his turn, watching the other children while he waited. Once his turn came Bilal reminded him that he needed to put an apron on. He refused to do this and became upset. Bilal was standing with her hands covered in paint and with other children waiting. Another practitioner observed what was happening and immediately stepped in to support Bilal. She reminded Haroon that Bilal had clearly said that an apron needed to be worn, she complimented him for waiting his turn so patiently and offered to help him put his apron on. Haroon agreed and went on to enjoy the activity with Bilal.

Consistency

All staff need to do the same thing as consistency is *the* key to positive behaviour in young children. A setting-wide approach to behaviour is fundamental to any organisation. Children need to know what is expected of them and all staff need to have a clear idea of how they can support children.

Outstanding settings are those whose staff have clear, effective strategies for managing behaviour which are applied consistently and understood by the children.

A good behaviour policy should ensure this happens. Remember we don't all have to agree on everything but being professional means compromising and agreeing to agree!

Being seen to be fair

Children need to see fairness happening – to do this successfully a consistent approach needs to be used with *all* the children (see above). Practitioners should never underestimate how closely children observe their behaviour. Children learn from those around them and mimic much adult behaviour.

Even the youngest children are passionate about fairness and practitioners need to set up strategies for themselves to use to ensure fairness. These may include:

▶ not making promises to children or parents that you can't keep;

▶ trying not to have favourites;

▶ being generous and equal with your time;

▶ using aids to ensure fairness, such as sand timers to give children equal time on shared equipment, e.g. bikes;

▶ listening to both sides of an argument;

▶ trying to facilitate and not referee (see example above).

An ounce of prevention – give positive attention before an incident occurs

This strategy works on the premise that most angry outbursts and undesirable behaviours are one way to get attention or cover up anxieties. Careful observation of individual children can reveal those activities which may trigger difficult behaviour. Thoughtful preparation for those activities can relieve the anxiety for children or provide them with the attention they need at a more appropriate time.

Example

Happy Days nursery school regularly has a weekly session with 'Tumble and Play', a group that comes to the nursery and sets up physical activities and works with small groups of children.

Every week Milo disrupts the group by running around, refusing to wait his turn, shouting, etc.

Farhana, Milo's key person, has come to dread these sessions and would like Milo to stop attending them. She has discussed this with her supervisor who has said that Milo *should* be included.

Farhana devised a plan to prepare Milo for these sessions.

▶ She asked the owners of 'Tumble and Play' for a leaflet/booklet about the group.

▶ She made a careful note during one of the activities of the content of the session.

▶ She brought her camera to work with her.

Before the session she did several things with Milo:

▶ She looked at the 'Tumble and Play' leaflet with him, reminding him of all the lovely equipment, etc. they had. She asked Milo if he would like to take the leaflet home to share with his parents.

▶ The day before the session she said to Milo, 'Let's practice some of the activities so we are ready for the "Tumble and Play" session.' She and Milo had fun practising tumbles, roly-polies, etc.

▶ At the end of the day she reminded Milo's mother that 'Tumble and Play' were coming the next day and said that she and Milo had a surprise in store for her.

▶ Before the 'Tumble and Play' session Farhana and Milo practised their activities again and agreed that Farhana would take some photographs of the session for Milo to share with his parents and family.

During the session Milo was on his best behaviour. He enjoyed showing the other children his tumbles and roly-polies. He was much admired and praised for his efforts by the 'Tumble and Play' staff.

Farhana took pictures of the session and sent some of them home with Milo. The rest were displayed in the setting.

Work in partnership with parents

Agree and share any strategies you are using with parents. Ask them what they do at home. Best practice is an agreed strategy that will be worked on or carried out both at school and at home.

Communication between parents and setting is crucial and can take many forms:

▶ a noticeboard that displays all setting policies including a behaviour policy;

▶ pastoral meetings either requested by the parents or the setting;

▶ informal daily chats (be aware of when and how these chats take place and remember to ensure privacy and confidentiality);

▶ a shared behaviour plan for an individual child that includes shared home/school targets and is regularly reviewed;

▶ a home/pre-school diary or boomerang books – note that entries about a child should always focus on positives and achievements;

▶ photographs sent home or even video clips (again be aware of issues of permission);

▶ e-mail or text messages to keep in touch with busy parents;

▶ telephone or mobile phone calls (always make sure the parent has time to talk before starting a conversation).

The EYFS Principles into Practice card 2.2 asks practitioners to consider:

How do you know parents understand the setting's policies on important areas such as learning and teaching, inclusion and behaviour? Have they been involved in drawing them up?

Share the challenge of difficult behaviour

Dealing with problematic behaviour can be demoralising for staff. Make sure that the whole staff team share the challenge of difficult behaviour – don't leave it all to the key person or to the setting SENCO. All staff in settings have a shared responsibility for all the children who attend the setting.

Try not to bargain with a child

Do not over-complicate interactions with a child by being drawn into bargaining with them, e.g. 'if you do this you can …' conversations. If you are clear in your expectations and what you are asking is reasonable, then you should expect a child to cooperate.

Remember that being consistent and clear is paramount to making children feel at ease and secure. If you feel you want to reward a child that is OK but try not to use the potential reward as a bribe to get a child to do something.

Make time to reflect after a difficult episode

After a difficult episode with a child or children it is good to have time to reflect and debrief.

▶ What has happened?

▶ How did it happen?

▶ How can it be avoided in the future?

Staff should never be left to go home in the evening upset about an occurrence that has happened during the day. Try to build a reflection time at the end of your session, even if it only lasts for 5–10 minutes.

Often practitioners need time to check out with colleagues.

Acknowledge considerate behaviour with a simple 'thank you'

Showing consideration and saying thank you goes a long way towards building better behaviour in any setting. This could be thanking your colleagues for supporting or listening to you, or thanking the children for sitting when you asked them to.

Hands-on activity

One of the most effective strategies to use with children to show you understand how they are feeling is **to acknowledge the feeling.** This may mean using phrases like, 'I can see that you are feeling … [angry, sad, cross, disappointed, worried, etc.].'

In a staff meeting/training consider what the effects of this may be in your setting.

Ask all members to try out the strategy for a week.

At your next staff meeting ask team members how it went and use this as a starting point for discussion on other strategies you can all try. (In doing this together as a team you begin to build a bank of strategies and effective practice.)

Top Tip

Write the phrase **'I can see that you are feeling …'** in big letters and place them high around the room as a reminder to staff.

Further reading

Drifte, Collette (2008) *Encouraging Positive Behaviour in the Early Years: A Practical Guide*, 2nd edn. Sage.

Swale, Jason (2006) *Setting the Scene for Positive Behaviour in the Early Years: A Framework for Good Practice*. Routledge.

CHAPTER SIX

Observing behaviour

> The aim of this chapter is to introduce a range of observational techniques which can support practitioners in observing behaviour.
>
> The chapter sets out:
>
> ▶ an overview of observation
>
> ▶ themed observations
>
> ▶ tracking observations
>
> ▶ ABC observations
>
> and includes:
>
> ▶ a Hands-on activity
>
> ▶ Further reading.

Observation is the single most powerful tool that practitioners have in order to gather information and evidence about a child's behaviour and to pinpoint their areas of strength and difficulty.

Once these observations are put together with all the other information we have about a child, we can begin to analyse and plan what needs to be done to best support that child. All early years settings have a system in place to observe and record children's progress. However, there are some children for whom more in-depth observation of their behaviour is needed.

The process is straightforward but not easy as there is a skill to observation which only comes with practice. All practitioners should have the chance to carry out extended observations to ensure that they develop this important skill.

Observing behaviour

Observing behaviour is frequently different to other observations because we often cannot plan our observation in the same way as we do others. Children do not always 'perform' just because we are observing them and sometimes we have to record what happened after the event.

It is important, however, that we record the information as if it was a planned observation, as this gives us an opportunity to properly analyse what has happened. The analysis is just as important when observing behaviour as it is for any other focus and the subsequent planning is crucial to effecting change.

Many children's behaviour will, on close examination, form a pattern. Once this pattern is recognised and understood steps can be taken to support the child to make better choices. *In many cases changing what happens before and after inappropriate behaviour is what changes the behaviour itself.*

Included here are three kinds of observation formats which can be useful when observing and recording behaviour.

A 'themed observation' sheet

This type of in-depth observation involves looking at children for a longer period of time, usually up to 20 minutes, and focusing on a particular area. Unlike a narrative observation, only the area of focus is recorded in the practitioner's notes (see page 69).

The observation needs to be carefully planned as you will need to be undisturbed by other children for up to 20 minutes. The support of other staff is essential – you may have to rearrange staff or enlist extra help in order to free yourself from normal duties. In some circumstances it will be necessary to 'set up' a particular game or activity which will provide you with the information that you need. Again this may involve another member of staff working with a group of children so that you can then observe.

Many settings have ways to show children that they should not be disturbed at this time. A badge or hat which indicates that you have 'special work' or 'writing' to do is very useful and children soon get used to this idea.

In this case everything connected to behaviour is focused on and written down in a narrative style. This is then analysed on the **follow-up** sheet (see page 70).

It is important to analyse your observation carefully and to reflect upon what you have seen. It is very helpful to have observations carried out by other members of staff as well which can then be discussed together. Having completed the follow-up sheet you should then have a list of significant points.

Check out your significant points with any other information you have about the child, including their strengths. This will help you to see your observations in terms of the whole child. You should refer back to the developmental guides to make sure that you have appropriate expectations. Remember, however, that these are not set in stone and each child's development may vary.

The significant points and conclusions you reach, having looked at the observations, should enable you to plan what needs to happen next.

A 'tracking observation' sheet

This helps us to focus on a child's movements and interactions around the setting. Sometimes behaviour is linked to lack of concentration and/or engagement with activities. It is important that we have a way of observing children's movements around the nursery to see if a pattern can be seen.

A tracking observation is one of the best ways to record this. It can tell you:

▶ which activities and areas a child spends the most time at;

▶ which activities or areas of the setting they avoid;

▶ the amount of time spent at any given activity;

▶ if they become engrossed in an activity;

▶ if they never settle to an activity;

▶ If they stay longer when adults are present;

▶ if they play alongside other children;

▶ if they move away when other children approach.

The information can be recorded in different ways, for example on a simple chart with space for noting down how long and where a child spends their time. Additional columns can be added if you wish to also record who the child was with or note their level of involvement (see page 71).

Alternatively some practitioners prefer a more visual method of recording and in this case a little preparation is necessary. This involves drawing a simple plan of the setting (see page 72) – the child's movements can then be mapped out by drawing lines between activities. The order of the activities is denoted by numbers and the amount of time – usually minutes – spent in each area is also noted.

With the information that is gained, practitioners can think more carefully about what they would like to observe in more detail or formulate further questions to ask about what might be happening for the child.

An 'ABC method' or 'before, during and after' sheet

Sometimes it is helpful to break down a behaviour observation into three areas as we write. This is also sometimes called the ABC method. It records the before, during and after of any incident in the nursery and is an excellent way of discovering patterns of behaviour.

A – meaning Antecedent or what happened **before.**
B – meaning Behaviour or what the child did **during** the incident.
C – meaning Consequence or what happened **after**.

Breaking down the behaviour in this way helps us to really think about what we have seen. The follow-up sheet helps us to ask ourselves the right sort of questions in order to plan what we need to do and how we can support the child.

On the following pages are examples of the formats for recording these types of observation. Both the observation and the follow-up sheets for the ABC method are annotated which will help you to complete your own observation. Blank copies of all the record sheets can be found on the CD-ROM.

Themed Observation Sheet

Child's name:	Date:
Focus of observation:	Observed by:

Time	

Themed Observation Follow-up Sheet

What was noticed

What this could tell us

What we should do next

Observed by: Discussed with:

Tracking Observation Sheet

Name of child:			DoB:	
Name of adult observing:			Date:	

Time	Activity/Area	Adults?	Children?	Involvement?

Tracking Observation – Setting Plan

Date:	Time started:	Time finished:
Name of child:		DoB:
Name of adult observing:		

Observing and Recording Behaviour Example Sheet

Before – putting it into context	During – recording the actual event	After – what happened next
Who, where, when and why?	**What?**	**And then?**
This is when we have the chance to put the behaviour into context. It can be very important when trying to establish whether or not there is a pattern forming.	This part of the observation is when we record what actually happened, e.g. what did the target child do – snatched a toy, pinched another child, threw a toy across the room?	We then need to look at what happened next for all those involved.
List details of *who* the target child was with at the time. Is it when a particular member of staff or child is with them? This can often reveal clashes of personality, another child who provokes or even show other children to be displaying equally inappropriate behaviour which we may not have noticed.	Note down what actions or words the target child used or displayed. This is important when we analyse what behaviour we want to change	What did the *target child* do next? Did they continue playing, did they seem upset, did they run away from the situation?
		What did the *other child* involved do? Did they retaliate, did they walk away, did they become upset?
Where the inappropriate behaviour occurs is another aspect to the observation. Is it always outside on the bikes, in the messy play area or on the carpet?		What did the *surrounding children* do? Did they call for an adult, did they become involved themselves, were they shocked or upset or unaware of what was happening?
Recording *when* a particular child displays inappropriate behaviour can prove very interesting. Is it always at the end of the morning, just before lunch, every Monday morning, when you are settling down for a story or at tidy-up time?		What did the *adults* do? Did they give the target child attention, did they ask for an explanation, did they comfort the other child, did they brush the incident aside?
Why – was there a *trigger?* For some children tiredness, hunger, being left first thing in the morning, having to sit for circle time or being asked to tidy up when they are engrossed in a game can be the *trigger* which sets them off.		By considering the consequences for all concerned we are able, in the follow-up analysis, to see what might have been a better outcome for all concerned.

 Building Better Behaviour in the Early Years, SAGE © Chris Dukes and Maggie Smith, 2009

Behaviour Follow-up Example Sheet
Analysing Your Observation

How could I have changed what happened before? How could I have prevented the trigger?	What behaviour do I want to change? What behaviour do I want to see instead?	What would have been a better consequence? What would I like to have happened instead?	What do I need to do now?
Look at the context in which the behaviour took place. Then you need to decide if there is anything that you could have changed to prevent the behaviour happening in the first place. If you have more than one observation you might see a pattern beginning to emerge. Sometimes there may be a very clear trigger for a particular behaviour. When you understand what this trigger is or can begin to see why a child behaved in a certain way you are half way to being able to support the child to change that behaviour.	It is usually easy to identify unacceptable behaviour. What you need to think about next is what you would prefer the child to do, given the same set of circumstances. It is important to have a very clear idea of what this is because you will need to have a plan to support the child to be able to make better choices in the future.	This involves you looking at what happened after the behaviour occurred and considering the actions of all those involved. It may be that on reflection the staff could have done something different which may have changed the outcome. Perhaps other children in the setting need some support or guidance as well as the target child.	Many settings will use either an Individual Education Plan or a Behaviour Support Plan. These record the target behaviours and the strategies which will be used to support a child.

 Building Better Behaviour in the Early Years, SAGE © Chris Dukes and Maggie Smith, 2009

Planning for behaviour needs

When planning for children's behaviour needs it is worth keeping at the forefront of our minds that sometimes the behaviour we are trying to change has been learnt over many months or even years. It should not therefore be an expectation that changes will be brought about quickly as this is most unlikely. Often challenging behaviour has its roots in deep-seated difficulties that we may not be aware of or in circumstances that we are unable to influence or change.

We should try to be optimistic but also realistic about what we can achieve, particularly in the short term. Often the hard work we put in to helping and supporting a child is only evident in improved behaviour when they have moved on into another setting or to school.

The key messages are as follows:

▶ **Consistency** – all members of staff and parents have to be rigorous in sticking to the same boundaries and using the same strategies. Children are experts at catching us when we are tired or in a hurry, in finding the weakest link on a staff team and in playing adults off against each other given the opportunity!

▶ **Patience** – it is only natural to get exasperated by some behaviour but we must try to keep calm and not expect overnight changes.

▶ **Perseverance** – this can be difficult when we get disheartened by a seeming lack of progress. Remember, however, that some children are so lacking in self-esteem that they deliberately push adults away and are waiting for us to 'give up on them'.

▶ **A positive attitude** – again this is sometimes difficult to maintain. It is helpful to look for even the slightest change, detach the behaviour from the child and 'catch the child being good' because no child is difficult all the time.

▶ **A sense of humour** – on some days this may be the only thing that keeps you going and is linked closely with the next point.

▶ **Essential team work** – discussing difficulties with supportive colleagues is crucial and dealing with any child's behaviour should be seen as everyone's responsibility.

▶ Last but not least is **time** – change of any sort takes time. Behaviour takes time to plan for, time to put strategies into place, time for them to take effect, time to become part of everyday practice, time before we see progress and then reap the benefits. It is worth remembering this when we judge either the child or ourselves too harshly.

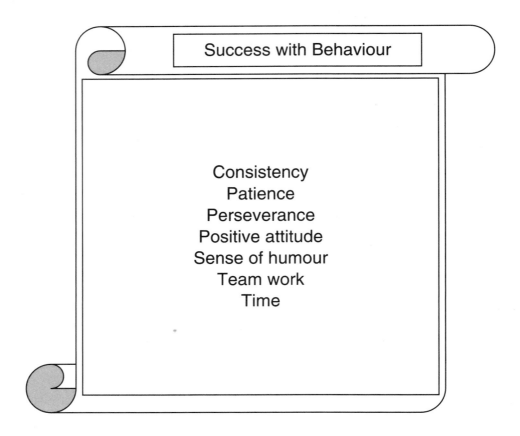

Many settings will use either a ***behaviour support plan*** or an ***individual education plan*** to record the target behaviours and strategies which will be used to support a child. Most settings are familiar with an individual education plan or IEP and a blank format is included on the CD-ROM.

What is a behaviour support plan?

A behaviour support plan is very much like an IEP but some practitioners prefer to use this format as it can be more focused.

▶ It deals specifically with behaviour issues.

▶ *All* staff would be expected to contribute to, be aware of and implement the plan.

▶ It is crucial that parents understand, contribute to and support the plan.

▶ It includes much more detailed information about strategies to be used at the setting and at home.

▶ It is reviewed and updated after short periods.

Behaviour Support Plan

Child's name:			Date of birth:
Adults involved in devising the plan: Parental involvement:			Date of plan: Date of review:
Original behaviour	Preferred behaviour	Strategies to be used by all staff	Outcome

Hands-on activity

1. Over a period of a few weeks try using each of the different types of observation on a particular child you don't know very well.

2. Compare the findings from each of the observations to see which one gives you the most helpful information.

3. Discuss your findings with the child's key person.

 Further reading

Dukes, Chris and Smith, Maggie (2009) *Recognising and Planning for Special Needs in the Early Years*. Sage Publications.

CHAPTER SEVEN

A skills bank

The aim of this chapter is to provide practitioners and parents with some skills, information and advice about important aspects of practice in relation to behaviour.

Each can be used as stand-alone leaflets to be shared or can be displayed on staff-room noticeboards. They can also be used as a starting point for team discussion or training.

The subject areas include:

- Attachment
- Being a Key Person
- Learning Styles
- Promoting Children's Independence
- Offering Choices
- Visual Timetables
- Supporting Children to Share
- Developing Positive Listening and Talking Skills
- Developing Good Body Language
- Circle Time
- Puppets and Persona Dolls
- 25 Ways to Say 'Well Done'
- 25 Ways to Build Self-Esteem
- Let's Talk About … Schemas
- Let's Talk About … Biting
- Let's Talk About … Swearing
- Let's Talk About … Tantrums

Points for Practitioners
Attachment

Attachment is a theory first suggested by John Bowlby in 1969. The theory says that babies are instinctively looking for secure attachments. This is in order to have their needs met and to seek comfort in being close, both physically and emotionally, to a small number of adults.

Q. What happens if babies and young children do not have secure attachments?

A. Research has shown that this can have far-reaching effects on all aspects of a child's development which can last into adulthood. These include extreme reactions, poor body awareness and poor ability to 'read' emotions or describe feelings. It can also lead to difficulties in forming close relationships.

Q. How can this affect a child's behaviour?

A. Some difficulties which can be associated with behaviour are poor attention, concentration or control, attention-seeking behaviours, lack of curiosity, empathy or remorse, lack of playfulness, little trust in adults and an inability to express emotions. In times of stress children can also exhibit bizarre or different behaviour.

Q. How has the theory of attachment affected early years practice?

A. Bowlby's theory prompted research by others and out of this in particular came the key person approach which is now considered to be an essential part of early years practice.

Q. What is the key person approach?

The key person approach is a way of working which enables and supports close attachments between individual children and individual practitioners. It is also one which encourages a close working relationship between the practitioner and the parent or carer.

Q. How does attachment affect a child's learning?

A. Again research has shown that the quality of a child's learning and the development of resilience can depend on the quality of their relationships both with their key person and their primary carers. The importance of a secure, sensitive, responsive and consistent relationship cannot be emphasised enough.

Points for Practitioners
Being a Key Person

> *A key person has special responsibilities for working with a small number of children, giving them the reassurance to feel safe and cared for and building relationships with their parents.*
>
> (EYFS Practice Guidance, page 15, para. 3.4)

How to support an individual child

- Be a positive behaviour role model
- Strive to build positive self-esteem in your key group children
- Help to raise individual children's 'positive profile' with other staff and children
- Value individual efforts and find different ways to say 'well done'
- Show genuine interest in the things children do and say
- Don't allow others to label a child as 'naughty'
- Share with your colleagues any positive strategies that have worked
- Work out what a child likes and share with colleagues
- Promote a child's strengths to your colleagues and make sure they are recorded in record-keeping
- Try to make some 'one-on-one' time every day with individual children to help children feel 'safe and cared for'

How to support parents/carers

- Make time each day to say hello and find something positive to say about their child
- Discuss issues sensitively and don't retell information or stories about a child to other parents
- Find an effective way to communicate with busy people, e.g. a boomerang book, text messages, e-mail, etc.
- Respect child-rearing practices different from your own
- Find shared objectives and work out a plan with parents to support individual children's behaviour
- Keep the relationship friendly and supportive but maintain your professionalism
- Be available to talk but make sure first you have the time – if not, agree a time with parents. This ensures you are prepared for any meeting

Points for Practitioners
Learning Styles

Successful practitioners know their children well. They can tell you about the interests of the child and can recognise a child's individual learning style.

How you can do this

1. You will learn about the interests of the child by **_observing_** what they like to do at your setting, and by **_talking_** to parents and the child himself/ herself about what they like to do at home.
2. Through observation you will be able to work out a child's learning style. Use the ideas below to help you.

Auditory learners may:

*   enjoy talking and explanations, e.g. like to express themselves
*   sometimes remember by talking out loud
*   like to have things explained, e.g. enjoy listening to adults
*   talk to themselves while learning something new
*   repeat new things they have learned, e.g. repeat what practitioner says during activities

Visual learners may:

*   remember visual details and enjoy stories with props or pictures
*   prefer to see what they are learning and enjoy seeing things work, e.g. watching worms, oil and water experiments, etc.
*   can have trouble following instructions, e.g. may need things broken down into single stages
*   respond to the use of visual timetables and diagrams, e.g. a daily calendar activity

Kinesthetic–tactile learners may:

*   prefer 'moving and doing' activities, e.g. outdoor play, dance and musical activities
*   want to always do whatever is being talked about, e.g. during a story stamp their feet
*   like to move around or 'fiddle' with something while listening or talking
*   often 'talk' with their hands
*   like to touch things in order to learn about them, sometimes snatch and grab

Use the insight you have gained to support and plan for a child's needs by incorporating interests and learning styles into planning and activities. This will go a long way to encouraging positive behaviour in your setting.

Points for Practitioners
Promoting Children's Independence

We have all heard children say 'I do', 'I can', 'Let me do it', 'I wanted to do that!' This is because young children have a strong desire to become independent.

Young children have a right to independence in the same way as we all do. Those children who are encouraged to be independent are less likely to become frustrated and will as a result behave better.

Learning how to be independent is an important part of the early years curriculum. Find below some tips for supporting children's independence.

Activities and equipment

- Let children choose their own activities and try to adopt a 'plan', 'do', 'review' approach, that is talk with children about what they would like to do, encourage and facilitate them to do it, and talk it over with them afterwards.

- Do not interfere with a child's activity/work/painting. Accept what they have created by themselves. Remember, 'it's the doing that counts'.

- Put equipment in low units so children can self select.

- Pictorially label all boxes so children know what is inside (cut pictures out of equipment catalogues).

- Put small amounts of equipment in boxes so that children can easily lift them.

- Allow children to work on a variety of surfaces, e.g. the floor, a low table, a tray, etc.

- Accept that a child may want to return to a piece of work so help them keep it safe until later in the session.

- Photograph completed activities, such as models, before children are asked to put equipment away.

Going outside

- Allow plenty of time for children to fetch and put on their outdoor coats/shoes, etc.

- Make time to show children how to put their own coats/shoes, etc. on.

- When helping a child with their coat always make sure they do the last bit themselves. This will give a child a feeling of satisfaction and pride, especially when praised for their efforts.

- Make sure every child has their own place to put their coat and shoes and that it is easily accessible.

- Try not to send all the children to get their coats at the same time!

Points for Practitioners
Offering Choices

What do we mean by offering choices?

This is when a child is encouraged by a practitioner or parent to select an object or an activity from two or more options, e.g. 'What book would you like me to read, *Winnie the Pooh* or *Brown Bear*?' 'Where would you like to sit? On the red chair or the green chair?' 'Would you like to play in the sand or in the water?', etc.

Why is this important for children?

Choice-making empowers children as it makes them feel that they have a say in what they are doing. This is important to all children and especially to those who sometimes demonstrate challenging behaviour.

Offering choice is also a useful tool for practitioners who can use the offer of a choice to make sure children do what is required of them, e.g. children comply with adults without being told specifically to do something.

Why is it a useful tool?

- All children need to learn to make choices as a life skill.

- Offering choice can be particularly useful when trying to get children to engage or participate in activities, e.g. a child who doesn't want to sit for a story or a child who never has a drink while at the setting, etc.

- Most children will choose between two options when previously they would not accept anything.

- It avoids conflict over small matters.

- It allows children to have a say in the day-to-day running of a setting.

The children who benefit most from being offered choices are:

- Those children who find selecting activities difficult.

- Those children who like to say 'no' to participation in nursery activities.

- Those children who often make a 'fuss' over small things, e.g. the colour of a cup.

- All children will benefit from being offered choices.

Points for Practitioners
Visual Timetables

A visual timetable is a pictorial way of showing children what is happening in their day. Young children have little sense of time, so a set of photographs, pictures or real objects to represent different activities or times of the day can be very helpful in showing the routine of the pre-school and the sequence of activities.

It can be used in many different ways:

- With the whole pre-school group as a reminder of what is happening throughout the day. It promotes independence and is particularly useful for 'change-over' times.

- With small groups who perhaps need the security and confidence of knowing what is happening next or who find it hard to choose activities.

- With individuals who have specific targets or need guiding between activities or help with concentration or behaviour.

Once you have a set of photographs or objects they can be:

- pinned on the wall

- hung on a washing line

- fixed onto card with Velcro strips

- put into a 'Talking photo album'

Useful tips

- Keep it simple.

- Planning and preparation is essential.

- Make sure that you have a clear purpose for using the timetable.

- Ensure that all staff understand how you intend it to be used.

- Make sure it is displayed at a child's eye level.

Points for Practitioners
Supporting Children to Share

Sharing is an important skill that children need to learn. It is one of the key roles of a practitioner to support children to share and take turns.

Children who are good at sharing are showing that they are aware of the needs of others. This in turn will lead to empathy with their peers. This is crucial if children are to go on to learn how to work cooperatively with both adults and their friends.

Ways in which practitioners can support children to learn to share

- Role model waiting patiently themselves.
- Limit waiting time for children, especially at going outside time, meal times and story times.
- During turn-taking games make sure every child has a turn at going first.
- Use positive language to praise children, e.g. 'I am impressed at how good you are at waiting for your turn.'
- Use puppets, circle time and story time to depersonalise situations that need to be talked about.
- Offer toys and activities that encourage social play rather than individual play.

Sharing activities and equipment and changing activities

Practitioners can ensure the fair sharing of equipment and activities by devising and implementing strategies that help children to wait for their turn. Try to find ways to allow children to help you monitor and use these strategies.

- Use a sand timer or lists and a stopwatch to share out desirable equipment like bikes or when using new equipment.
- Use arm bands or aprons to limit the number of children at a popular activity such as the home corner.
- Have a means to count down to change, e.g. 'We need to tidy up in five minutes.' Use a large kitchen clock with a timer or count children down verbally.
- Support children to finish off their game by offering a suggestion as to how they might do this.
- Allow children to put an activity away for later – consider having a 'not finished yet' or 'work in progress' shelf.
- If equipment must be put away and a child is upset by this offer to take a photograph of what they have made for them to keep or to display or take home (this offers children a way out of a situation – one of the 25 strategies).

Points for Practitioners
Developing Positive Listening and Talking Skills

Practitioners are at the front line when it comes to communicating and listening to young children. Most practitioners are interested in the children in their care. However, they are also always busy usually with lots of different things to do in a working day. They way practitioners listen to and communicate with children is perhaps the most import factor in building better pre-school behaviour.

Below are some tips on **listening and talking** to children.

Listening

- Make the *time and space* to listen to young children – more difficult than it sounds in a busy room. Plan for regular quiet times, a quiet or listening corner and one-on-one times.
- Give your *full attention* to children when they talk to you – that may mean stopping what you are doing.
- Bend down to *eye level* with the child and give them your full attention.
- *Acknowledge children's contribution* during busy story sessions by giving them a smile, a nod or a thumbs up sign.
- When a child is talking to you nod and *make eye contact* in the same way that you would when talking to an adult.
- Do not *interrupt* or 'talk for' a child – give them the time and space to speak for themselves.

Talking

- *Acknowledge* the child's feeling, e.g. 'I can see you are upset.'
- *Reflect back* what you think the child has said to you, especially if the child is involved in a dispute with another child, e.g. 'So you think that … took the bike before your turn was over.'
- Use *open questions,* e.g. 'tell me …', 'what can I do to help?', 'what should we do now?' 'how does that feel?', etc.
- Make *positive statements* instead of negatives or don't dos, e.g. 'try to keep the water in the tray' instead of 'don't splash water all over the floor'.
- Use *I statements* to help make it clear that it is the behaviour you don't like not the child, e.g. 'I don't like kicking' instead of 'I don't like you when you kick.'
- Sound calm, clear and controlled when dealing with any behaviour issues. That way children know what to expect.
- Use a *child's name* when offering praise. This allows others to hear and is a positive for those who usually only hear their name being used when being told off.
- Be *specific* when using praise. That way children know what the praise is for, e.g. 'Well done, Jack, for lining up so sensibly.'

Points for Practitioners
Developing Good Body Language

Non-verbal messages are important to all humans but children are especially tuned into the messages conveyed by body language.

Body language occurs subconsciously but those movements often convey a powerful message to the person or child we are interacting with.

The dos and don'ts tips outlined below will help practitioners to become more aware of the signals they are conveying to children.

Do

- Be aware of yourself and the image you are projecting.
- Think how your face in particular looks to a child – is it looking angry or sad? Try not to look scary!
- Adopt an open palm posture with your arms held slightly out (a totally non-aggressive and non-challenging stance). This is very useful, especially if a child is angry.
- Try to maintain eye contact – but make sure it is not intrusive or staring.
- Get down to the child's level so he/she can make eye contact with you.
- Give your full attention.
- Nod your head when a child is talking to you or say 'mmmm …' – this shows them you are listening.
- Try to have a relaxed open posture.

Don't

- Stand with your hands on you hips or your arms folded. This looks very disapproving.
- Show shock on your face, even if you are shocked at what you may hear.
- Be distracted by other things that are happening in the room.
- Hold your hands or fists clenched tight.
- Scowl – try to relax your face.
- Sigh or look bored.
- Stand or sit too close – be aware of the child's personal space.
- Tower over a child – get down to their level.
- Move too quickly towards a child unless they are in danger.

The main point is to be aware of the messages you are conveying to the child through your body language. This will allow you to communicate better with a child and more importantly a child to communicate better with you.

Points for Practitioners
Circle Time

Circle time supports children to share their play and learning with each other. The beauty of the circle is that it allows children to see and hear everyone else. All that is needed is a comfortable floor space which is free from obstacles such as toys or furniture or any other distractions.

Circle time is when young children can develop their sense of belonging and become an active member of the pre-school community.

Things to remember

- Some children will find it hard and practitioners may need to offer one-to-one support and guidance.

- Practitioners should remember that children should not be expected to sit in one place listening for more than a few minutes.

- Those children who find it hard to do will often initially watch circle time from afar or be offered alternative activities until they are ready to join the group.

The benefits of circle time

Children are encouraged to:

- listen and follow instructions

- develop empathy

- build confidence when speaking

- learn to read non-verbal signs

- modify their use of tone and voice, e.g. whispering

- learn new words

- respond to story and rhyme

- share their personal experience

- raise their self-esteem

- consider big themes, e.g. friendship

- learn the language of feelings, sharing, etc.

- emulate the positive behaviour of adults and their peers.

Points for Practitioners
Puppets and Persona Dolls

Puppets can be made from almost anything and the success of any puppet depends on the skill with which a practitioner uses it.

Persona dolls are special larger dolls that can be used in much the same way as a puppet but can often be given a life of their own by practitioners and children together. These dolls and puppets can become a character that belongs in your pre-school with their own personality, background stories and family, likes and dislikes, just like another child.

The benefits of using puppets and persona dolls

- Through stories and conversations with the character children who need to find a voice to express their feelings can begin to talk.

- Children can 'find a friend' and someone to confide in.

- Children can begin to explore the language of feelings and emotions.

- Practitioners can recreate scenarios and incidents that have occurred in order to discuss them without personalising or labelling particular children.

- Children can learn to listen to each other through the dolls.

- Children can develop empathy with the dolls.

Ideas to try

- Take photographs of your puppets in everyday dilemmas such as playing and sharing. Use these as discussion points with the children.

- Use the puppets to introduce new language connected with themes such as friendship and sharing.

- Separate some puppets that can only be used by practitioners with children. This helps to keep them special.

- Have a system which can enables children to take turns in caring for the puppet – this will help to develop empathy and consideration.

- Create a bag to go with the puppets which contains some of their belongings such as a brush, face cloth, picture book, etc.

- Consider allowing the children to take the puppet home. This allows some children to show their emerging social skills with their parents.

25 Ways to Say 'Well Done'

1. You're a star

2. You're doing great

3. You have some great ideas

4. Fantastic job

5. I couldn't have done better myself

6. You don't give up, do you?

7. That was quick thinking

8. That's a beautiful job

9. What a brilliant idea

10. Good thinking

11. I'm really impressed

12. You've really got the hang of this

13. It's a pleasure to see you …

14. That was great problem-solving

15. What a good try

16. Superb

17. You are on top form today

18. Well remembered

19. You've done really well

20. You've really stuck with that

21. You have picked that up really quickly

22. It's a pleasure to see you working (or sharing) so well

23. How creative (or imaginative, or fast … etc.) you are

24. Whew! You are really busy today

25. What a brainwave

 Building Better Behaviour in the Early Years, SAGE © Chris Dukes and Maggie Smith, 2009

25 Ways to Build Self-Esteem

1. Provide an environment that is welcoming and stable.

2. Have a sharing or circle time every day.

3. Provide praise and encouragement to *all* children.

4. Provide for the individual needs of every child and view a child holistically.

5. Notice and comment on every small step of progress a child makes.

6. Send messages home about children's success.

7. Show individual children you value and respect them.

8. Have a special display board to celebrate new things children have learned.

9. Use children's names when talking to them.

10. Get down to the child's level and make eye contact when you speak to them.

11. Give a lot of genuine praise and show an interest in the things a child likes and does. Sincere interest often goes down better than praise.

12. Always look for the positives in a child and build on them. Think of them as their 'pathway to the future'.

13. Include children in the decisions that are made throughout the day at your setting, e.g. by offering choices.

14. Encourage children to ask you questions and involve you, e.g. 'Let's look at how this works'. 'Let's talk about the park before we go there', etc.

15. Provide clear boundaries for a child.

16. Support children to build realistic achievable goals.

17. When discussing an issue never bring up previous difficulties.

18. Don't compare children.

19. Support a child's problem-solving and decision-making skills.

20. Think about each child as an individual.

21. Provide an environment where children can take chances and try new things out.

22. Nurture the children in your care – remember how important you are to them.

23. Conditionally accept a child and let them know that.

24. Keep a sense of perspective and a sense of humour.

25. Ensure building positive self-esteem is a whole-setting issue and is incorporated into the setting's ethos and policies.

Let's Talk About....   **Schemas**

Q.   **What is a schema?**
A.   A schema is an interest in something with actions which are repeated over and over again in an observable pattern of behaviour. Through this babies and children develop their awareness of the world and so deepen their learning.

Q.   **How do schemas develop?**
A.   Schemas develop in clusters and link together in networks. In babies and toddlers schemas are based in the senses and in movement.
      As children get older the schemas in children's brains become more complex and coordinated. They can 'pretend' and also explore why things happen.

Q.   **Do all children have schemas?**
A.   Yes, all children have schemas, including children with special educational needs. Children's schemas are influenced by their experiences and environment, by people, objects and culture.

Q.   **What kinds of schemas are there and what might they look like?**
A.   There are many kinds of schemas. Some of the most common are:
      • connection – joining things like train tracks or using string or ribbons;
      • envelopment – covering or wrapping things up or making dens;
      • trajectories – lining up objects or moving to and fro (horizontal);
      • building towers, pouring, throwing, jumping up and down (vertical);
      • transporting – carrying things or pushing prams and carts;
      • scattering – spreading small objects around, stamping in puddles.

Q.   **Why is it important for parents and practitioners to know about schemas?**
A.   A good knowledge and understanding will help parents and practitioners to recognise a child's schema. Once recognised a schema can be tapped into in order to develop the child's learning. It also can inform planning and resourcing. When not understood schemas can be labelled as 'bad behaviour', e.g. children with a trajectory schema may be exploring throwing things but doing so inappropriately.

Biting

Q. Why does my child bite?

A. There are many reasons why a child bites and these can change depending on what age/stage they are at. Some children bite because they are frustrated, some bite because they are copying another child or a sibling while others may be seeking your attention because of the reaction they get if they bite.

Q. Is my child the only one that bites?

A. No, biting is common and many children bite some time during their childhood. But all children who do bite will eventually stop.

Q. What can I do if my child bites me?

A. Stay calm, show your disapproval by putting the child down or moving away. If he/she has hurt you say, 'Stop that, I don't like it. We do not bite.' Aim to be calm and in control while showing your child that you think their behaviour is unacceptable. Try not to make too much of a fuss and move on from the incident.

Q. My child bites his siblings and the other children at the pre-school. What should I do?

A. Observe your child to see when this is happening. Supervise your child closely and remove them from any situations that you think might lead to a biting episode before it happens.

Q. What should I do when my child bites another child?

A. Immediately remove the child who has done the biting to one side and give your attention to the other child. Once you have comforted the bitten child turn to the biter and say, 'No, we do not bite.' Make sure the biter does not receive any positive attention for biting (even if he/she cries). Then turn and move away (hard I know).

How to help a child who bites

- If a child manages a situation without biting acknowledge that by saying, 'I can see you are cross but you didn't hit or bite – well done.'

- Stay calm and in control.

- Be consistent in how you deal with a situation.

- Support the child to find other ways of dealing with frustration.

- Use puppets and stories to talk about how unpleasant biting is – depersonalise the situation.

- Never bite a child back or encourage another child to bite back.

If despite your efforts biting continues beyond the age of three discuss with a health professional or your area SENCO (with parental permission).

Swearing

Q. Why does my child use swear words?
A. Your child is using swear words because he/she has heard them being used by others and because he/she has received mixed messages about their use. Perhaps he/she has heard others, usually adults or older children, using these words, or perhaps the child has seen adults smile or appear shocked when they have used a swear word in the past.

Q. How can I deal with my child using these words?
A. Before dealing with swearing the adults around the child, especially the parents, should talk about their own attitude to swearing, e.g. what they think is OK and what they don't want to hear from their child. Once adults are clear about what is unacceptable it is easier then to convey this message to children.

Q. If my child uses a swear word what should I do?
A. Do not laugh/smile or look shocked or overreact (difficult we know) but instead try to:

- acknowledge the feeling, e.g. 'I can see that you are really cross/upset/fed up … but'

- say firmly, 'We do not use that word and I don't want to hear it again …'

- if the child says it again try your hardest to ignore them and pretend you didn't hear it

- then say, 'I know a better word for you to use …' (provide the child with an alternative).

Remember

- Children learn to use words from the adults around them.

- Adults should try not to overreact to a child swearing.

- Young children are fascinated by words – they enjoy using and learning new ones! So be careful what you say.

- Acknowledge the feeling behind the swearing but be firm in rejecting the words used.

- Help a child find alternative words to use.

- Most 3- and 4-year-olds go through a phase of saying rude phrases rather than swear words, e.g. 'You're a big bottom.'

 **Let's Talk About...**   **Tantrums**

Q.   What is a tantrum?
A.   A tantrum is when a young child usually aged between one and four loses control and cries and screams or shouts. Some children lie on the floor kicking or can throw things; some may hit and try to bite those around them. (Tantrums can be worse when a child is around two – hence the term 'terrible twos'.)

Q.   What causes a tantrum?
A.   Usually the child is frustrated and is unable to explain themselves, or sometimes it is when the child wants something and an adult has said no.

Q.   How does the child feel when having a tantrum?
A.   The child feels out of control, angry and usually scared.

Q.   Are tantrums inevitable?
A.   Sometimes yes, but often they can be anticipated and prevented by a practitioner or parent.

Q.   How can a practitioner or parent help avoid tantrums?
A.   • By working out when a tantrum usually happens and changing the circumstances so they can be avoided (an ounce of prevention).
      • By distracting the child before the tantrum gets hold.
      • By discussing the behaviour with the child after the tantrum has happened (usually later in the day and not immediately after the tantrum) and together trying to find new strategies for the child to use the next time they feel the same way.

Q.   What can I do when a child is having a tantrum?
A.   • Try not to be overwhelmed and stay calm and in control.
      • Acknowledge the child's feelings, e.g. 'I can see that you are really angry.'
      • Try to distract the child.
      • Keep the child and others safe. (This may mean removing the child, others or even furniture or equipment.)
      • Hold the child if you think that will help. (Use your judgement here as sometimes it can make things worse.)
      • Once the tantrum is over hug the child. (Remember, they have probably frightened themselves.)
      • After the event repeat that you could see that they were very angry **but** the tantrum behaviour was unacceptable.
      • Some time later talk about what they child could do the next time they feel the same way.

If tantrums do not lessen as the child gets older discuss with other team members and the child's parents. It may be agreed that further advice should be sought from a health visitor, your area SENCO/inclusion officer or the child's GP. (Of course you may proceed only with parental permission.)

Contacts and useful organisations

Chris Dukes and Maggie Smith (authors of Hands on Guides)

www.earlymatters.co.uk

National Early Years Network

77 Holloway Road
London
N7 8JZ
Tel: 020 7607 9597

Netmums

124 Mildred Avenue
Watford
WD18 7DX
www.netmums.com

ParentsCentre

www.parentscentre.gov.uk

SureStart

www.surestart.gov.uk

References

Call, Nicola (2003) *The Thinking Child Resource Book,* The Early Years Series. Network Educational Press.

Department for Education and Employment (2001) *Special Educational Needs: Code of Practice.* DfEE.

Department for Education and Skills (2007) *Statutory Framework for the Early Years Foundation Stage.* DfES.

Department for Education and Skills (2008) *Practice Guidance For the Early Years Foundation Stage.* DfES.

Donaldson, Margaret (1986) *Children's Minds.* HarperCollins.

Dowling, Marion (2005*) Young Children's personal, Social and Emotional Development,* 2nd edn. Paul Chapman Publishing.

Drifte, Colette (2008) *Encouraging Positive Behaviour in the Early Years: A Practical Guide,* 2nd edn. Sage.

Dukes, Chris and Smith, Maggie (2009) *Recognising and Planning for Special Needs in the Early Years.* Sage.

Glenn, Angela, Cousins, Jacquie and Helps, Alicia (2004) *Behaviour in the Early Years*. David Fulton.

National Children's Bureau Enterprise Ltd (2003) *Early Years and the Disability Discrimination Act 1995: What Service Providers Need to Know.* NCB.

Paige-Smith, Alice and Craft, Anna (2006) *Reflective Practice in the Early Years.* Open University Press.

Porter, Louise (2003) *Young Children's Behaviour: Practical Approaches for Caregivers and Teachers.* Paul Chapman Publishing.

Swale, Jason (2006) *Setting the Scene for Positive Behaviour in the Early Years: A Framework for Good Practice.* Routledge.

Visser, Jo (2007) *Supporting Personal, Social and Emotional Development*, Everything Early Years How To ... Series. Everything Early Years.

Index

EH40/2005 Workplace exposure limits

Containing the list of workplace exposure limits for use with the Control of Substances Hazardous to Health Regulations 2002 (as amended)

HSE Books

EH40/2005 contains material of different legal status.

Table 1 of EH40/2005 and the Notices of Approval have a special legal status as they are approved by the Health and Safety
Commission. The Control of Substances Hazardous to Health Regulations 2002 impose requirements by reference to these
sections, which are therefore legally binding. Thus, if Table 1 or the Notices of Approval apply to your work activities, health
and safety inspectors will expect you to be complying with these requirements, and will if necessary take appropriate
enforcement action.

The remainder of EH40/2005 is guidance. This guidance is issued by the Health and Safety Executive. Following the
guidance is not compulsory and you are free to take other action. But if you do follow the guidance you will normally be
doing enough to comply with the law. Health and safety inspectors seek to secure compliance with the law and may refer to
this guidance as illustrating good practice.

Contents

Foreword

The new OEL framework

This edition of EH40 represents a new departure for the setting of, and compliance with, occupational exposure limits (OELs). The previous system, setting OELs as maximum exposure limits (MELs) and occupational exposure standards (OESs) has been discontinued in favour of a single type of OEL known as the workplace exposure limit or WEL.

MELs and OESs were introduced in 1989, when the first Control of Substances Hazardous to Health Regulations (COSHH) came into force. The Control of Substances Hazardous to Health (Amendment) Regulations 2004[1] removed the definitions of these two types of OEL and replaced them with the definition of a WEL. These changes came into effect on 6 April 2005.

The changes came about as a result of concerns expressed by the Health and Safety Commission's Advisory Committee on Toxic Substances (ACTS) about how well employers and other stakeholders understood OELs, and about how widely these were being used in industry. Research carried out for HSE showed that those concerns were justified. As a result, an ACTS Working Group was given the task of considering a new approach to the setting and use of OELs.

A discussion document published in March 2002 set out the concerns with the existing system and proposed options for a new system.

Following the comments received on this discussion document, a formal Consultative Document was published in October 2003, which made proposals for a new OEL framework. These proposals included the introduction of eight principles of good practice for the control of exposure to substances hazardous to health, and replacing MELs and OESs with WELs. Responses to this Consultative Document showed strong support for these proposals. Paragraphs 5 and 6 of this publication provide information on the principles of good practice and on how to apply WELs.

A further aspect of the new framework is that certain former OESs have not been converted to WELs because of doubts that the limit was not soundly-based. Those OESs, for which there was some concern that health was not adequately protected at the value of the OES, have been removed. Details of these substances can be found in a table on the HSE website (http://www.hse.gov.uk/aboutus/hsc/meetings/2004/091104/c06c.pdf). This table also provides advice on whether *COSHH essentials*[2] can be used to obtain advice on the control of these substances.

Although only the courts can give an authoritative interpretation of law, in considering the application of this guidance to people working under another's direction, the following should be considered. If people working under the control and direction of others are treated as self-employed for tax and national insurance purposes they may nevertheless be treated as their employees for health and safety purposes. It may therefore be necessary to take appropriate action to protect them. If any doubt exists about who is responsible for the health and safety of a worker this could be clarified and included in the terms of a contract. However, remember, a legal duty under section 3 of the Health and Safety at Work (HSW

Act) cannot be passed on by means of a contract and there will still be duties towards others under section 3 of the HSW Act. If such workers are employed on the basis that they are responsible for their own health and safety, legal advice should be sought before doing so.

Introduction

1   Many people are exposed to a variety of substances at work (eg chemicals, fumes, dusts, fibres) which can, under some circumstances, have a harmful effect on their health. These are called 'hazardous substances'. If exposure to a hazardous substance is not properly controlled it may cause ill health in a number of ways. The substance may cause harm by too much being taken into the body through breathing, by being absorbed through the skin, by being swallowed, or by acting directly on the body at the point of contact, eg the skin. Some illnesses caused by exposure to hazardous substances in the workplace (occupational diseases) may not appear until a long time after the first exposure. Therefore, it is important to know in advance how to protect the health of people working with hazardous substances and also of other people who may be affected by the work being carried out. WELs for hazardous substances at work are set by the Health and Safety Commission (HSC) on the recommendations of its Advisory Committee on Toxic Substances (ACTS) and published in EH40. A more detailed explanation is on pages 37-38.

What are WELs?

2   WELs are occupational exposure limits (OELs) set under COSHH,[3] in order to help protect the health of workers. WELs are concentrations of hazardous substances in the air, averaged over a specified period of time referred to as a time-weighted average (TWA). Two time periods are used: long term (8 hours) and short term (15 minutes). Short-term exposure limits (STELs) are set to help prevent effects, such as eye irritation, which may occur following exposure for a few minutes.

WELs and COSHH

3   The first requirement of COSHH is to prevent exposure to substances hazardous to health where it is 'reasonably practicable' (ie the costs in reducing exposure would not be grossly disproportionate to the benefits). This can be achieved by:

■   changing the process so that the substance is no longer used/produced;
■   replacing it with a safer alternative; or
■   completely enclosing the process.

4   Regulation 7(7) of COSHH states that, 'without prejudice to the requirement to prevent exposure, control of exposure to a substance hazardous to health shall only be treated as adequate if -
  (a)   the principles of good practice for the control of exposure to substances hazardous to health set out in Schedule 2A are applied;
  (b)   any workplace exposure limit approved for that substance is not exceeded; and
  (c)   for a substance—
    (i)   which carries the risk phrase R45, R46 or R49, or for a substance or process which is listed in Schedule 1; or
    (ii)   which carries the risk phrase R42 or R42/43, or which is listed in section C of HSE publication *Asthmagen? Critical assessments of the evidence for agents implicated in occupational asthma*[4] as updated from

time to time, or any other substance which the risk assessment has shown to be a potential cause of occupational asthma, exposure is reduced to as low a level as is reasonably practicable'.

Principles of good practice for the control of exposure to substances hazardous to health

5   The eight principles of good practice for the control of exposure to substances hazardous to health are set out in Schedule 2A of *The Control of Substances Hazardous to Health Regulations 2002 (as amended). Approved Code of Practice and guidance.*[5] The principles are reproduced below:

(a)   design and operate processes and activities to minimise emission, release and spread of substances hazardous to health;

(b)   take into account all relevant routes of exposure – inhalation, skin absorption and ingestion – when developing control measures;

(c)   control exposure by measures that are proportionate to the health risk;

(d)   choose the most effective and reliable control options which minimise the escape and spread of substances hazardous to health;

(e)   where adequate control of exposure cannot be achieved by other means, provide, in combination with other control measures, suitable personal protective equipment;

(f)   check and review regularly all elements of control measures for their continuing effectiveness;

(g)   inform and train all employees on the hazards and risks from the substances with which they work and the use of control measures developed to minimise the risks;

(h)   ensure that the introduction of control measures does not increase the overall risk to health and safety.

6   If employers apply the principles correctly, exposure should be below any relevant WEL. Control by personal protective equipment should only be used when other measures are not reasonably practicable. The list of WELs applies to concentrations of hazardous substances breathed in by the worker and are used to determine the adequacy of control measures. There are several publications which give advice and guidance on what is required under the COSHH Regulations. Some useful references are given on page 55.

Inhaled substances not assigned WELs

7   The absence of a substance from the list of WELs does not indicate that it is safe. For these substances, exposure should be controlled to a level to which nearly all the working population could be exposed, day after day at work, without adverse effects on health. As part of the assessment required under regulation 6 of COSHH,

employers should determine their own working practices, and in-house standards for control. In some cases there may be sufficient information to set a self-imposed working standard, eg from manufacturers and suppliers of the substance, from publications of industry associations, occupational medicine and hygiene journals. Further information may be found in *Monitoring strategies for toxic substances*[6] and *COSHH essentials.*[2]

Employees and the self-employed

8   There are also some duties for employees and the self-employed under COSHH. Guidance is given in associated ACOPs, particularly the COSHH ACOP.[5] If a person working under an employer's control and direction is treated as self-employed for tax and national insurance purposes, they may nevertheless be an employee for health and safety purposes. You may need therefore to take appropriate action to protect them.

9   If you do not wish to employ workers on this basis, you should seek legal advice. Ultimately each case can only be decided on its own merits by a court of law.

Data Protection Act

10   Employers, in complying with the requirements of regulation 10 of COSHH, may decide to hold health surveillance records on their employees. The Data Protection Act[7] places requirements on those who hold personal data such as health surveillance records. Further information on the Act is available from the Office of the Information Commissioner (Tel: 01625 545745 Website: http://www.informationcommissioner.gov.uk/).

European occupational exposure limits

11   The exposure limits listed in Table 1 of this publication are all British limits, set under COSHH. In some cases, these also reflect a European limit applicable in all EU Member States. These limits were known originally as Indicative Limit Values (ILVs), and are currently called Indicative Occupational Exposure Limit Values (IOELVs).

12   IOELVs are health-based limits set under the Chemical Agents Directive (98/24/EC). The European Commission is advised on limits by its Scientific Committee on Occupational Exposure Limits (SCOEL). This committee evaluates the scientific information available on hazardous substances and makes recommendations for the establishment of an IOELV. IOELVs are listed in Directives, which Member States are obliged to implement by introducing national limits for the substances listed.

13   Only one IOELV Directive has so far been implemented, and the 63 limits arising from it are contained in Table 1.

14   Additionally, three limits in Table 1 derive from the Carcinogens Directive (2004/37/EC). These are the limits for benzene, hardwood dusts and vinyl chloride monomer, and are binding limits. Member States are obliged to implement binding limits exactly or to establish a national limit that is lower.

Further information and advice

15   Scientific and technical information for some of the substances listed in EH40 can be found in Toxicity Reviews, Criteria Documents and Risk Assessment Documents published by HSE and in the documents accompanying other nations' lists. [8-10] In addition, the scientific and technical basis for WELs set through the WATCH/ACTS process since the introduction of COSHH is published in EH64 *Summary criteria for occupational exposure limits.*[11] WELs that were established prior to the introduction of COSHH may not have an accompanying EH64 summary.

16   Further advice on occupational exposure limits and other aspects of occupational health and safety can be obtained from:

- HSE's Infoline: Tel 0845 345 0055
  Fax: 02920 859260
  e-mail: hseinformationservices@natbrit.com

- the HSE website: www.hse.gov.uk

- HSE local offices - the telephone numbers are listed in the telephone directory under 'Health and Safety Executive'.

HSE publications are available from HSE Books,
PO Box 1999, Sudbury, Suffolk CO10 2WA
(Tel: 01787 881165, Fax: 01787 313995,
Website: www.hsebooks.co.uk).

List of workplace exposure limits (WELs)

Annotations

BMGV Biological Monitoring Guidance Values are listed in Table 2.

Carc Capable of causing cancer and/or heritable genetic damage. The identified substances include those which:

- are assigned the risk phrases 'R45: May cause cancer'; 'R46: May cause heritable genetic damage'; 'R49: May cause cancer by inhalation' in the *Approved supply list*;[12] or
- a substance or process listed in Schedule 1 of COSHH.

Sen Capable of causing occupational asthma. The identified substances are those which:

- are assigned the risk phrase 'R42: May cause sensitisation by inhalation'; or 'R42/43: May cause sensitisation by inhalation and skin contact' in the *Approved supply list*; or
- are listed in section C of HSE publication *Asthmagen? Critical assessments of the evidence for agents implicated in occupational asthma*[4] as updated from time to time, or any other substance which the risk assessment has shown to be a potential cause of occupational asthma.

Sk Can be absorbed through skin. The assigned substances are those for which there are concerns that dermal absorption will lead to systemic toxicity.

The system of nomenclature for the substances listed below is based, in the main, on the convention adopted by the International Union of Pure Applied Chemistry (IUPAC). Where this is not the case the substances will be flagged:

- **INN** International Non-proprietary Name;

- **ISO** International Organisation for Standardisation.

Notes

1   For the purposes of these limits, respirable dust and inhalable dust are those fractions of the airborne dust which will be collected when sampling is undertaken in accordance with the methods described in MDHS14/3 *General methods for sampling and gravimetric analysis of respirable and inhalable dust*,[13] as amended by the ISO/CEN convention.

2   Where no specific short-term exposure limit is listed, a figure three times the long-term exposure limit should be used.

3   The tables reproduce the R-phrases from the *Approved supply list*.[12]

4   Substances marked with an asterisk* indicate those for which classification and labelling was introduced in the 29th Adaptation to Technical Progress of the European Community's Dangerous Substances Directive.

Risk phrases from the Chemicals (Hazard Information and Packaging for Supply) Regulations 2002 used in EH40

R2	Risk of explosion by shock, friction, fire or other sources of ignition
R4	Forms very sensitive explosive metallic compounds
R5	Heating may cause an explosion
R6	Explosive with or without contact with air
R7	May cause fire
R8	Contact with combustible material may cause fire
R10	Flammable
R11	Highly flammable
R12	Extremely flammable
R14	Reacts violently with water
R16	Explosive when mixed with oxidising substances
R17	Spontaneously flammable in air
R19	May form explosive peroxides
R20	Harmful by inhalation
R20/21	Harmful by inhalation and in contact with skin
R20/21/22	Harmful by inhalation, in contact with skin and if swallowed
R20/22	Harmful by inhalation and if swallowed
R21	Harmful in contact with skin
R21/22	Harmful in contact with skin and if swallowed
R22	Harmful if swallowed
R23	Toxic by inhalation
R23/24	Toxic by inhalation and in contact with skin
R23/25	Toxic by inhalation and if swallowed
R23/24/25	Toxic by inhalation, in contact with skin and if swallowed
R24	Toxic in contact with skin
R24/25	Toxic in contact with skin and if swallowed
R25	Toxic if swallowed
R26	Very toxic by inhalation
R26/27/28	Very toxic by inhalation, in contact with skin and if swallowed
R26/28	Very toxic by inhalation and if swallowed
R27	Very toxic in contact with skin
R27/28	Very toxic in contact with skin and if swallowed
R28	Very toxic if swallowed
R29	Contact with water liberates toxic gas
R31	Contact with acids liberates toxic gas
R32	Contact with acids liberates very toxic gas
R33	Danger of cumulative effects
R34	Causes burns
R35	Causes severe burns
R36	Irritating to eyes
R36/37	Irritating to eyes and respiratory system
R36/37/38	Irritating to eyes, respiratory system and skin
R36/38	Irritating to eyes and skin
R37	Irritating to respiratory system
R37/38	Irritating to respiratory system and skin
R38	Irritating to skin
R39	Danger of very serious irreversible effects
R39/23/24/25	Toxic: danger of very serious irreversible effects through inhalation, in contact with skin and if swallowed
R40	Limited evidence of a carcinogenic effect
R41	Risk of serious damage to eyes
R42	May cause sensitisation by inhalation
R42/43	May cause sensitisation by inhalation and skin contact
R43	May cause sensitisation by skin contact
R44	Risk of explosion if heated under confinement

R45	May cause cancer
R46	May cause heritable genetic damage
R48	Danger of serious damage to health by prolonged exposure
R48/20	Harmful: danger of serious damage to health by prolonged exposure through inhalation
R48/20/21	Harmful: danger of serious damage to health by prolonged exposure through inhalation and in contact with skin
R48/20/21/22	Harmful: danger of serious damage to health by prolonged exposure through inhalation, in contact with skin and if swallowed
R48/20/22	Harmful: danger of serious damage to health by prolonged exposure through inhalation and if swallowed
R48/22	Harmful: danger of serious damage to health by prolonged exposure if swallowed
R48/23	Toxic: danger of serious damage to health by prolonged exposure through inhalation
R48/23/24	Toxic: danger of serious damage to health by prolonged exposure through inhalation and in contact with skin
R48/23/25	Toxic: danger of serious damage to health by prolonged exposure through inhalation and if swallowed
R48/23/24/25	Toxic: danger of serious damage to health by prolonged exposure through inhalation, in contact with skin and if swallowed
R48/25	Toxic: danger of serious damage to health by prolonged exposure if swallowed
R49	May cause cancer by inhalation
R50	Very toxic to aquatic organisms
R50/53	Very toxic to aquatic organisms, may cause long-term adverse effects in the aquatic environment
R51	Toxic to aquatic organisms
R51/53	Toxic to aquatic organisms, may cause long-term adverse effects in the aquatic environment
R52/53	Harmful to aquatic organisms, may cause long-term adverse effects in the aquatic environment
R53	May cause long-term adverse effects in the aquatic environment
R59	Dangerous for the ozone layer
R60	May impair fertility
R61	May cause harm to the unborn child
R62	Possible risk of impaired fertility
R63	Possible risk of harm to the unborn child
R65	Harmful: may cause lung damage if swallowed
R66	Repeated exposure may cause skin dryness or cracking
R67	Vapours may cause drowsiness and dizziness
R68	Possible risk of irreversible effects

Table 1: List of approved workplace exposure limits

This list is legally binding, as it reproduces the list of workplace exposure limits (WELs) which have been approved by the Health and Safety Commission. The limits are given in ppm and mg.m^{-3}. The conversion method is given on page 42. The Control of Substances Hazardous to Health Regulations 2002 impose requirements by reference to this list.

However, the entries in the columns headed 'CAS number', and 'Comments' are not part of the approved list of WELs. The workplace exposure limits of the dusts included in the list below refer to the inhalable dust fraction, unless otherwise stated.

Table 1: List of approved workplace exposure limits

Substance	CAS number	Workplace exposure limit				Comments
		Long-term exposure limit (8-hour TWA reference period)		Short-term exposure limit (15-minute reference period)		
		ppm	mg.m⁻³	ppm	mg.m⁻³	
Acetaldehyde	75-07-0	20	37	50	92	R12, 36/37, 40
Acetic anhydride	108-24-7	0.5	2.5	2	10	R10, 20/22, 34
Acetone	67-64-1	500	1210	1500	3620	R11 36, 66, 67
Acetonitrile	75-05-8	40	68	60	102	R11, 20/21/22, 36
o-Acetylsalicylic acid	50-78-2	-	5	-	-	
Acrylaldehyde (Acrolein)	107-02-8	0.1	0.23	0.3	0.7	R11 24/25, 26, 34, 50
Acrylamide	79-06-1	-	0.3	-	-	Carc Sk R45, 46, 20/21, 25, 36/38, 43, 48/23/24/25, 62
Acrylonitrile	107-13-1	2	4.4	-	-	Carc Sk R45, 11, 23/24/25, 37/38, 41, 43, 51/53* HSC/E plans to review the limit values for this substance
Allyl alcohol	107-18-6	2	4.8	4	9.7	Sk R10, 23/24/25, 36/37/38, 50
Aluminium alkyl compounds		-	2	-	-	R14, 17, 34
Aluminium metal	7429-90-5					
inhalable dust		-	10	-	-	
respirable dust		-	4	-	-	
Aluminium oxides	1344-28-1					
inhalable dust		-	10	-	-	
respirable dust		-	4	-	-	
Aluminium salts, soluble		-	2	-	-	
2-Aminoethanol	141-43-5	3	7.6	6	15	R20/21/22, 34*
Ammonia, anhydrous	7664-41-7	25	18	35	25	R10, 23, 34, 50*
Ammonium chloride, fume	12125-02-9	-	10	-	20	R22, 36
Ammonium sulphamidate	7773-06-0	-	10	-	20	
Aniline	62-53-3	1	4	-	-	Sk R23/24/25, 40, 41, 48/23/24/25, 68, 50*
Antimony and compounds except stibine (as Sb)		-	0.5	-	-	
p-Aramid respirable fibres	26125-61-1	0.5 fibres/ml		-	-	

Arsenic and arsenic
  compounds except
  arsine (as As)
		-	0.1	-	-	Carc
						HSC/E plans to review the limit values for this substance

Arsine	7784-42-1	0.05	0.16	-	-	R12, 26, 48/20, 50/53
Asphalt, petroleum fumes	8052-42-4	-	5	-	10	
Azodicarbonamide	123-77-3	-	1.0	-	3.0	Sen R42, 44

Substance	CAS number	Workplace exposure limit				Comments
		Long-term exposure limit (8-hour TWA reference period)		Short-term exposure limit (15-minute reference period)		
		ppm	mg.m^{-3}	ppm	mg.m^{-3}	
Barium compounds, soluble (as Ba)		-	0.5	-	-	
Barium sulphate	7727-43-7					
inhalable dust		-	10	-	-	
respirable dust		-	4	-	-	
Benzene	71-43-2	1	-	-	-	Carc Sk R45, 46, 11, 36/38, 48/23/24/25, 65*
Benzyl butyl phthalate	85-68-7	-	5	-	-	R61, 62, 50/53*
Benzyl chloride	100-44-7	0.5	2.6	1.5	7.9	Carc R45, 22, 23, 37/38, 41, 48/22
Beryllium and beryllium compounds (as Be)		-	0.002	-	-	Carc
Bis(2-ethylhexyl) phthalate	117-81-7	-	5	-	10	R60, 61
Bis(chloromethyl) ether	542-88-1	0.001	0.005	-	-	Carc R45, 10, 22, 24, 26
Bornan-2-one	76-22-2	2	13	3	19	
Boron tribromide	10294-33-4	-	-	1	10	R14, 26/28, 35
Bromacil (ISO)	314-40-9	1	11	2	22	
Bromine	7726-95-6	0.1	0.66	0.3	2	R26, 35, 50
Bromomethane	74-83-9	5	20	15	59	Sk R23/25, 36/37/38, 48/20, 68, 50, 59
Butane	106-97-8	600	1450	750	1810	Carc (only applies if Butane contains more than 0.1% of buta-1, 3-diene) R12
Buta-1,3-diene	106-99-0	10	22	-	-	Carc R45, 46, 12 HSC/E plans to review the limit values for this substance
Butan-1-ol	71-36-3	-	-	50	154	Sk R10, 22, 37/38, 41, 67
Butan-2-ol	78-92-2	100	308	150	462	R10, 36/37, 67
Butan-2-one (methyl ethyl ketone)	78-93-3	200	600	300	899	Sk BMGV R11, 36, 66, 67
2-Butoxyethanol	111-76-2	25	-	50	-	Sk BMGV R20/21/22, 36/38
2-Butoxyethyl acetate	112-07-2	20	-	50	-	Sk R20/21
n-Butyl acrylate	141-32-2	1	5	5	26	R10, 36/37/38, 43
n-Butyl chloroformate	592-34-7	1	5.7	-	-	R10, 23, 34
sec-Butyl acetate	105-46-4	200	966	250	1210	R11, 66
tert-Butyl acetate	540-88-5	200	966	250	1210	R11, 66
Butyl acetate	123-86-4	150	724	200	966	R10, 66, 67
Butyl lactate	138-22-7	5	30	-	-	

Substance	CAS number	Workplace exposure limit				Comments
		Long-term exposure limit (8-hour TWA reference period)		Short-term exposure limit (15-minute reference period)		
		ppm	mg.m⁻³	ppm	mg.m⁻³	
2-sec-Butylphenol	89-72-5	5	31	-	-	Sk
Cadmium & cadmium compounds except cadmium oxide fume, cadmium sulphide & cadmium sulphide pigments (as Cd)		-	0.025	-	-	Carc (cadmium metal,* cadmium chloride, flouride and sulphate)
Cadmium oxide fume (as Cd)	1306-19-0	-	0.025	-	0.05	Carc R45, 26, 48/23/25, 62, 63, 68, 50/53*
Cadmium sulphide and cadmium sulphide pigments (respirable dust as Cd)		-	0.03	-	-	Carc (cadmium sulphide*)
Caesium hydroxide	21351-79-1	-	2	-	-	
Calcium carbonate	1317-65-3					
inhalable dust		-	10	-	-	
respirable		-	4	-	-	
Calcium cyanamide	156-62-7	-	0.5	-	1	R22, 37, 41
Calcium hydroxide	1305-62-0	-	5	-	-	
Calcium oxide	1305-78-8	-	2	-	-	
Calcium silicate	1344-95-2					
inhalable dust		-	10	-	-	
respirable		-	4	-	-	
Captan (ISO)	133-06-2	-	5	-	15	R23, 40, 41, 43, 50
Carbon black	1333-86-4	-	3.5	-	7	
Carbon dioxide	124-38-9	5000	9150	15000	27400	
Carbon disulphide	75-15-0	10	32	-	-	Sk R11, 36/38, 48/23, 62, 63 HSC/E plans to review the limit values for this substance
Carbon monoxide	630-08-0	30	35	200	232	Bmgv R12, 23, 48/23, 61
Carbon tetrachloride	56-23-5	2	13	-	-	Sk R23/24/25, 40, 48/23, 52/53, 59*
Cellulose	9004-34-6					
inhalable dust		-	10	-	20	
respirable		-	4	-	-	
Chlorine	7782-50-5	0.5	1.5	1	2.9	R23, 36/37/38, 50
Chlorine dioxide	10049-04-4	0.1	0.28	0.3	0.84	R6, 8, 26, 34, 50*
Chloroacetaldehyde	107-20-0	-	-	1	3.3	R24/25, 26, 34, 40, 50*
2-Chloroacetophenone	532-27-4	0.05	0.32	-	-	
Chlorobenzene	108-90-7	1	-	3	-	Sk R10, 20, 51/53*
Chlorodifluoromethane	75-45-6	1000	3590	-	-	
Chloroethane	75-00-3	50	-	-	-	R12, 40, 52/53
2-Chloroethanol	107-07-3	-	-	1	3.4	Sk R26/27/28

Substance	CAS number	Workplace exposure limit				Comments
		Long-term exposure limit (8-hour TWA reference period)		Short-term exposure limit (15-minute reference period)		
		ppm	mg.m^{-3}	ppm	mg.m^{-3}	
1-Chloro-2,3-epoxypropane (Epichlorohydrin)	106-89-8	0.5	1.9	1.5	5.8	Carc R45, 10, 23/24/25, 34, 43
Chloroform	67-66-3	2	9.9	-	-	Sk R22, 38, 40, 48/20/22
Chloromethane	74-87-3	50	105	100	210	R12, 40, 48/20
1-Chloro-4-nitrobenzene	100-00-5	-	1	-	2	Sk R23/24/25, 40, 48/20/21/22, 68, 51/53*
Chlorosulphonic acid	7790-94-5	-	1	-	-	R14, 35, 37
Chlorpyrifos (ISO)	2921-88-2	-	0.2	-	0.6	Sk R25, 50/53*
Chromium	7440-47-3	-	0.5	-	-	
Chromium (II) compounds (as Cr)		-	0.5	-	-	
Chromium (III) compounds (as Cr)		-	0.5	-	-	
Chromium (VI) compounds (as Cr)		-	0.05	-	-	Carc, Sen* BMGV
Cobalt and cobalt compounds (as Co)		-	0.1	-	-	Carc (cobalt dichloride and sulphate) Sen

Copper
  fume
  dusts and mists (as Cu)
	7440-50-8	-
		-
			0.2
			1
				-
				-
					-
					2	

Cotton dust	See page 29	-	2.5	-	-	
Cryofluorane (INN)	76-14-2	1000	7110	1250	8890	
Cumene	98-82-8	25	125	50	250	Sk R10, 37, 65, 51/53
Cyanamide	420-04-2	-	2	-	-	R21, 25, 36/38, 43
Cyanides, except HCN, cyanogen & cyanogen chloride		-	5	-	-	Sk
Cyanogen chloride	506-77-4	-	-	0.3	0.77	
Cyclohexane	110-82-7	100	350	300	1050	R11, 38, 65, 67, 50/53*
Cyclohexanol	108-93-0	50	208	-	-	R20/22, 37/38
Cyclohexanone	108-94-1	10	-	20	-	Sk BMGV R10, 20
Cyclohexylamine	108-91-8	10	41	-	-	R10, 21/22, 34
2,4-D (ISO)	94-75-7	-	10	-	20	R22, 37, 41, 43, 52/53
Dialkyl 79 phthalate	83968-18-7	-	5	-	-	
Diallyl phthalate	131-17-9	-	5	-	-	R22, 50/53*
Diatomaceous earth, natural, respirable dust	61790-53-2	-	1.2	-	-	
Dibenzoyl peroxide	94-36-0	-	5	-	-	R2, 36, 43
Dibismuth tritelluride	1304-82-1	-	10	-	20	
Diboron trioxide	1303-86-2	-	10	-	20	
1,2-Dibromoethane (Ethylene dibromide)	106-93-4	0.5	3.9	-	-	Carc, Sk R45, 23/24/25, 36/37/38, 51/53*

Substance	CAS number	Workplace exposure limit				Comments
		Long-term exposure limit (8-hour TWA reference period)		Short-term exposure limit (15-minute reference period)		
		ppm	mg.m^{-3}	ppm	mg.m^{-3}	
Dibutyl hydrogen phosphate	107-66-4	1	8.7	2	17	
Dibutyl phthalate	84-74-2	-	5	-	10	R61, 62, 50
Dichloroacetylene	7572-29-4	-	-	0.1	0.39	R2, 40, 48/20
1,2-Dichlorobenzene (ortho-dichlorobenzene)	95-50-1	25	153	50	306	Sk R22, 36/37/38, 50/53*
1,4-Dichlorobenzene (para-dichlorobenzene)	106-46-7	25	153	50	306	R36, 40, 50/53*
1,3-Dichloro-5,5-dimethyl-hydantoin	118-52-5	-	0.2	-	0.4	
1,1-Dichloroethane	75-34-3	100	-	-	-	Sk R11, 22, 36/37, 52/53*
1,2-Dichloroethane (Ethylene dichloride)	107-06-2	5	21	-	-	Carc, Sk R45, 11, 22, 36/37/38
1,2-Dichloroethylene, cis:trans isomers 60:40	540-59-0	200	806	250	1010	R11, 20, 52/53*
Dichlorofluoromethane	75-43-4	10	43	-	-	
Dichloromethane	75-09-2	100	350	300	1060	Bmgv Sk R40 HSC/E plans to review the limit values for this substance
2,2'-Dichloro-4,4'-methylene dianiline (MbOCA)	101-14-4	-	0.005	-	-	Carc Sk Bmgv R45, 22, 50/53
Dicyclohexyl phthalate	84-61-7	-	5	-	-	
Dicyclopentadiene	77-73-6	5	27	-	-	R11, 20/22, 36/37/38 51/53
Diethylamine	109-89-7	10	30	25	76	R11, 20/21/22, 35
Diethyl ether	60-29-7	100	310	200	620	R12, 19, 22, 66, 67
Diethyl phthalate	84-66-2	-	5	-	10	
Diethyl sulphate	64-67-5	0.05	0.32	-	-	Carc Sk R45, 46, 20/21/22, 34
Dihydrogen selenide (as Se)	7783-07-5	0.02	-	0.05	-	R23/25, 33
Diisobutyl phthalate	84-69-5	-	5	-	-	
Diisodecyl phthalate	26761-40-0	-	5	-	-	
Diisononyl phthalate	28553-12-0	-	5	-	-	
Diisooctyl phthalate	27554-26-3	-	5	-	-	
Diisopropylamine	108-18-9	5	21	-	-	R11, 20/22, 34
Diisopropyl ether	108-20-3	250	1060	310	1310	R11, 19, 66, 67
N,N-Dimethylacetamide	127-19-5	10	36	20	72	Sk BMGV R20/21, 61
N,N-Dimethylaniline	121-69-7	5	25	10	50	Sk R23/24/25, 40, 51/53
N,N-Dimethylethylamine	598-56-1	10	30	15	46	R12, 20/22, 34
Dimethoxymethane	109-87-5	1000	3160	1250	3950	
Dimethylamine	124-40-3	2	3.8	6	11	R12, 20, 37/38, 41
2-Dimethylaminoethanol	108-01-0	2	7.4	6	22	R10, 20/21/22, 34

Substance	CAS number	Workplace exposure limit				Comments
		Long-term exposure limit (8-hour TWA reference period)		Short-term exposure limit (15-minute reference period)		
		ppm	mg.m^{-3}	ppm	mg.m^{-3}	
Dimethyl ether	115-10-6	400	766	500	958	R12
Dimethylformamide	68-12-2	10	30	20	61	Sk R61, 20/21, 36
2,6-Dimethylheptan-4-one	108-83-8	25	148	-	-	R10, 37
Dimethyl phthalate	131-11-3	-	5	-	10	
Dimethyl sulphate	77-78-1	0.05	0.26	-	-	Carc Sk R45, 25, 26, 34, 43, 68*
Dinitrobenzene, all isomers	25154-54-5	0.15	1	0.5	3.5	Sk R26/27/28, 33, 50, 53
Dinonyl phthalate	84-76-4	-	5	-	-	
1,4-Dioxane	123-91-1	25	91	100	366	Sk R11, 19, 36/37, 40, 66
Diphenylamine	122-39-4	-	10	-	20	R23/24/25, 33, 50/53
Diphenyl ether (vapour)	101-84-8	1	7.1	-	-	
Diphosphorus pentasulphide	1314-80-3	-	1	-	3	R11, 20/22, 29, 50
Diphosphorus pentoxide	1314-56-3	-	-	-	2	R35
Diquat dibromide (ISO)	85-00-7	-	0.5	-	1	R22, 26, 36/37/38, 43, 48/25, 50/53
Disodium disulphite	7681-57-4	-	5	-	-	R22, 31, 41
Disodium tetraborate, anhydrous	1330-43-4	-	1	-	-	
Disodium tetraborate, decahydrate	1330-96-4	-	5	-	-	
Disodium tetraborate, pentahydrate	11130-12-4	-	1	-	-	
Disulphur dichloride	10025-67-9	-	-	1	5.6	R14, 20, 25, 29, 35, 50
2,6-Di-*tert*-butyl-*p*-cresol	128-37-0	-	10	-	-	
6,6'-Di-tert-butyl-4,4'-thiodi-*m*-cresol	96-69-5	-	10	-	20	
Diuron (ISO)	330-54-1	-	10	-	-	R22, 40, 48/22, 50/53
Emery	1302-74-5					
inhalable dust		-	10	-	-	
respirable		-	4	-	-	
Endosulfan (ISO)	115-29-7	-	0.1	-	0.3	Sk R24/25, 36, 50/53
Enflurane	13838-16-9	50	383	-	-	
Ethane-1,2-diol	107-21-1					Sk
particulate		-	10	-	-	R22
vapour		20	52	40	104	
Ethanethiol	75-08-1	0.5	1.3	2	5.2	R11, 20, 50/53
Ethanol	64-17-5	1000	1920	-	-	R11
2-Ethoxyethanol	110-80-5	10	37	-	-	Sk R10, 20/21/22, 60, 61 HSC/E plans to review the limit values for this substance
2-Ethoxyethyl acetate	111-15-9	10	55	-	-	Sk R20/21/22, 60, 61

Substance	CAS number	Workplace exposure limit				Comments
		Long-term exposure limit (8-hour TWA reference period) ppm	mg.m⁻³	Short-term exposure limit (15-minute reference period) ppm	mg.m⁻³	
2-Ethylhexyl chloroformate	24468-13-1	1	8	-	-	-
Ethyl acetate	141-78-6	200	-	400	-	R11, 36, 66, 67
Ethyl acrylate	140-88-5	5	21	15	62	R11, 20/21/22, 36/37/38, 43
Ethylamine	75-04-7	2	3.8	6	11	R12, 36/37
Ethylbenzene	100-41-4	100	441	125	552	Sk R11, 20
Ethyl chloroformate	541-41-3	1	4.5	-	-	R11, 22, 26, 34
Ethyl cyanoacrylate	7085-85-0	-	-	0.3	1.5	R36/37/38
Ethyl formate	109-94-4	100	308	150	462	R11, 20/22, 36/37
Ethylene oxide	75-21-8	5	9.2	-	-	Carc R45, 46, 12, 23, 36/37/38
4-Ethylmorpholine	100-74-3	5	24	20	96	Sk
Ferrous foundry particulate inhalable dust	See page 29	-	10	-	-	
respirable dust		-	4	-	-	
Flour dust	See page 30	-	10	-	30	Sen HSC/E plans to review the limit values for this substance
Fluoride (inorganic as F)	16984-48-8	-	2.5	-	-	
Fluorine	7782-41-4	1	-	1	-	R7, 26, 35
Formaldehyde	50-00-0	2	2.5	2	2.5	R23/24/25, 34, 40, 43 HSC/E plans to review the limit values for this substance
Formamide	75-12-7	20	37	30	56	R61
Formic acid	64-18-6	5	9.6	-	-	R35
2-Furaldehyde (furfural)	98-01-1	2	8	5	20	Sk R21, 23/25, 36/37, 40
Germane	7782-65-2	0.2	0.64	0.6	1.9	
Glutaraldehyde	111-30-8	0.05	0.2	0.05	0.2	Sen R23/25, 34, 42/43, 50
Glycerol, mist	56-81-5	-	10	-	-	
Grain dust	See page 30	-	10	-	-	Sen
Graphite inhalable dust	7440-44-0	-	10	-	-	
respirable		-	4	-	-	
Gypsum inhalable dust	10101-41-4	-	10	-	-	
respirable		-	4	-	-	

Substance	CAS number	Workplace exposure limit				Comments
		Long-term exposure limit (8-hour TWA reference period)		Short-term exposure limit (15-minute reference period)		
		ppm	mg.m^{-3}	ppm	mg.m^{-3}	
Halogeno-platinum compounds (complex co-ordination compounds in which the platinum atom is directly co-ordinated to halide groups) (as Pt)	See page 30	-	0.002	-	-	Sen
Halothane	151-67-7	10	82	-	-	
Hardwood dust	See page 31	-	5	-	-	Carc Sen HSC/E plans to review the limit values for this substance
n-Heptane	142-82-5	500	-	-	-	R11, 38, 65, 67, 50/53
Heptan-2-one	110-43-0	50	237	100	475	Sk R10, 20/22
Heptan-3-one	106-35-4	35	166	100	475	Sk R10, 20, 36
n-Hexane	110-54-3	20	72	-	-	R11, 38, 48/20, 62, 65, 67, 51/53*
1,6-Hexanolactam	105-60-2					R20/22, 36/37/38
dust only		-	1	-	3	
dust and vapour		-	10	-	20	
Hexan-2-one	591-78-6	5	21	-	-	Sk R10, 48/23, 62, 67
Hydrazine	302-01-2	0.02	0.03	0.1	0.13	Carc Sk R45, 10, 23/24/25, 34, 43, 50/53
Hydrogen bromide	10035-10-6	-	-	3	10	R35, 37
Hydrogen chloride (gas and aerosol mists)	7647-01-0	1	2	5	8	R23, 35
Hydrogen cyanide	74-90-8	-	-	10	11	Sk R12, 26, 50/53
Hydrogen fluoride (as F)	7664-39-3	1.8	1.5	3	2.5	R26/27/28, 35
Hydrogen peroxide	7722-84-1	1	1.4	2	2.8	R5, 8, 20/22, 35*
Hydrogen sulphide	7783-06-4	5	7	10	14	R12, 26, 50
Hydroquinone	123-31-9	-	0.5	-	-	R22, 40, 41, 43, 68, 50
4-Hydroxy-4-methylpentan-2-one	123-42-2	50	241	75	362	R36
2-Hydroxypropyl acrylate	999-61-1	0.5	2.7	-	-	Sk R23/24/25, 34, 43
2,2'-Iminodi(ethylamine)	111-40-0	1	4.3	-	-	Sk R21/22, 34, 43
Indene	95-13-6	10	48	15	72	
Indium and compounds (as In)		-	0.1	-	0.3	
Iodine	7553-56-2	-	-	0.1	1.1	R20/21, 50
Iodoform	75-47-8	0.6	9.8	1	16	
Iodomethane	74-88-4	2	12	-	-	Sk R21, 23/25, 37/38, 40

Substance	CAS number	Workplace exposure limit				Comments
		Long-term exposure limit (8-hour TWA reference period)		Short-term exposure limit (15-minute reference period)		
		ppm	mg.m^{-3}	ppm	mg.m^{-3}	
Iron oxide, fume (as Fe)	1309-37-1	-	5	-	10	
Iron salts (as Fe)		-	1	-	2	
Isobutyl acetate	110-19-0	150	724	187	903	R11, 66
Isocyanates, all (as -NCO)		-	0.02	-	0.07	Sen HSC/E plans to review the limit values for this substance
Isoflurane	26675-46-7	50	383	-	-	
Isooctyl alcohol (mixed isomers)	26952-21-6	50	271	-	-	
Isopropyl acetate	108-21-4	-	-	200	849	R11, 36, 66, 67
Isopropyl chloroformate	108-23-6	1	5.1	-	-	
Kaolin, respirable dust	1332-58-7	-	2	-	-	
Ketene	463-51-4	0.5	0.87	1.5	2.6	
Limestone	1317-65-3					
total inhalable		-	10	-	-	
respirable		-	4	-	-	
Liquefied petroleum gas	68476-85-7	1000	1750	1250	2180	Carc (only applies if LPG contains more than 0.1% of buta-1, 3-diene) R12
Lithium hydride	7580-67-8	-	0.025	-	-	
Lithium hydroxide	1310-65-2	-	-	-	1	
Magnesite	546-93-0					
inhalable dust		-	10	-	-	
respirable dust		-	4	-	-	
Magnesium oxide (as Mg)	1309-48-4					
inhalable dust		-	10	-	-	
fume and respirable dust		-	4	-	-	
Malathion (ISO)	121-75-5	-	10	-	-	Sk R22, 50/53*
Maleic anhydride	108-31-6	-	1	-	3	Sen R22, 34, 42/43
Manganese and its inorganic compounds		-	0.5	-	-	
Marble	1317-65-3					
total inhalable		-	10	-	-	
respirable		-	4	-	-	
Mercaptoacetic acid	68-11-1	1	3.8	-	-	R23/24/25, 34
Methacrylic acid	79-41-4	20	72	40	143	R21/22, 35
Methacrylonitrile	126-98-7	1	2.8	-	-	Sk R11, 23/24/25, 43*
Methanethiol	74-93-1	0.5	1.0	-	-	R12, 23, 50/53*
Methanol	67-56-1	200	266	250	333	Sk R11, 23/24/25, 39/23/24/25

Substance	CAS number	Workplace exposure limit				Comments
		Long-term exposure limit (8-hour TWA reference period)		Short-term exposure limit (15-minute reference period)		
		ppm	mg.m^{-3}	ppm	mg.m^{-3}	
2-Methoxyethanol	109-86-4	5	16	-	-	Sk R10, 20/21/22, 60, 61
2-Methoxyethyl acetate	110-49-6	5	25	-	-	Sk R20/21/22, 60, 61
(2-methoxymethylethoxy) propanol	34590-94-8	50	308	-	-	Sk
1-Methoxypropan-2-ol	107-98-2	100	375	150	560	Sk R10
1-Methoxypropyl acetate	108-65-6	50	274	100	548	Sk R10, 36
Methyl acetate	79-20-9	200	616	250	770	R11, 36, 66, 67
3-Methylbutan-1-ol	123-51-3	100	366	125	458	
Methyl cyanoacrylate	137-05-3	-	-	0.3	1.4	R36/37/38
4,4'-Methylenedianiline	101-77-9	0.01	0.08	-	-	Carc Sk Bmgv R45, 39/23/24/25, 43, 48/20/21/22, 68, 51/53
Methyl ethyl ketone peroxides (MEKP)	1338-23-4	-	-	0.2	1.5	
Methyl methacrylate	80-62-6	50	208	100	416	R11, 37/38, 43
2-Methylcyclohexanone	583-60-8	50	233	75	350	R10, 20
Methylcyclohexanol	25639-42-3	50	237	75	356	
N-Methylaniline	100-61-8	0.5	2.2	-	-	Sk R23/24/25, 33, 50/53
5-Methylheptan-3-one	541-85-5	10	-	20	-	R10, 36/37
5-Methylhexan-2-one	110-12-3	20	95	100	475	Sk R10, 20
2-Methylpentane-2,4-diol	107-41-5	25	123	25	123	R36/38
4-Methylpentan-2-ol	108-11-2	25	106	40	170	Sk R10, 37
4-Methylpentan-2-one	108-10-1	50	208	100	416	Sk Bmgv R11, 20, 36/37, 66
2-Methylpropan-1-ol	78-83-1	50	154	75	231	R10, 37/38, 41, 67
2-Methylpropan-2-ol	75-65-0	100	308	150	462	R20
1-Methyl-2-pyrrolidone	872-50-4	25	103	75	309	Sk R36/38
Methyl-tert-butyl ether	1634-04-4	25	92	75	275	R11, 38*
Mica	12001-26-2					
total inhalable		-	10	-	-	
respirable		-	0.8	-	-	
MMMF (Machine-made mineral fibre) (except for Refractory Ceramic Fibres and Special Purpose Fibres)		5 mg.m^{-3} and 2 fibres/millilitre		-	-	HSC/E plans to review the limit values for this substance
Molybdenum compounds (as Mo)						
soluble compounds		-	5	-	10	
insoluble compounds		-	10	-	20	
Monochloroacetic acid	79-11-8	0.3	1.2	-	-	Sk R25, 34, 50

Substance	CAS number	Workplace exposure limit				Comments
		Long-term exposure limit (8-hour TWA reference period) ppm / mg.m⁻³		Short-term exposure limit (15-minute reference period) ppm / mg.m⁻³		
		ppm	mg.m⁻³	ppm	mg.m⁻³	
Morpholine	110-91-8	20	72	30	109	Sk R10, 20/21/22, 34
Nickel and its inorganic compounds (except nickel tetracarbonyl): water-soluble nickel compounds (as Ni)		-	0.1	-	-	Sk Carc (nickel oxides and sulphides) Sen (nickel sulphate)
nickel and water-insoluble nickel compounds (as Ni)		-	0.5	-	-	
Nicotine	54-11-5	-	0.5	-	1.5	Sk R25, 27, 51/53
Nitric acid	7697-37-2	2	5.2	4	10	R8, 35
Nitrobenzene	98-95-3	1	5.1	2	10	Sk R23/24/25, 40, 48/23/24, 62, 51/53
Nitromethane	75-52-5	100	254	150	381	R5, 10, 22
2-Nitropropane	79-46-9	5	19	-	-	Carc R45, 10, 20/22
Nitrous oxide	10024-97-2	100	183	-	-	
Orthophosphoric acid	7664-38-2	-	1	-	2	R34
Osmium tetraoxide (as Os)	20816-12-0	0.0002	0.002	0.0006	0.006	R26/27/28, 34
Oxalic acid	144-62-7	-	1	-	2	R21/22
2,2'-Oxydiethanol	111-46-6	23	101	-	-	R22
Ozone	10028-15-6	-	-	0.2	0.4	
Paracetamol, inhalable dust	103-90-2	-	10	-	-	
Paraffin wax, fume	8002-74-2	-	2	-	6	
Paraquat dichloride (ISO), respirable dust	1910-42-5	-	0.08	-	-	R24/25, 26, 36/37/38, 48/25, 50/53
Pentacarbonyliron (as Fe)	13463-40-6	0.01	0.08	-	-	
Pentaerythritol	115-77-5					
inhalable dust		-	10	-	20	
respirable dust		-	4	-	-	
Pentan-2-one	107-87-9	200	716	250	895	
Pentan-3-one	96-22-0	200	716	250	895	R11, 37, 66, 67
Pentyl acetates (all isomers)		50	270	100	541	R10, 66
2-Phenylpropene	98-83-9	50	246	100	491	R10, 36/37, 51/53*
Phenol	108-95-2	2	-	-	-	Sk R23/24/25, 34, 48/20/21/22, 68*
p-Phenylenediamine	106-50-3	-	0.1	-	-	Sk R23/24/25, 36, 43, 50/53
Phorate (ISO)	298-02-2	-	0.05	-	0.2	Sk R27/28, 50/53
Phosgene	75-44-5	0.02	0.08	0.06	0.25	R26, 34
Phosphine	7803-51-2	-	-	0.3	0.42	R12, 17, 26, 34, 50*

Substance	CAS number	Workplace exposure limit				Comments
		Long-term exposure limit (8-hour TWA reference period)		Short-term exposure limit (15-minute reference period)		
		ppm	mg.m^{-3}	ppm	mg.m^{-3}	
Phosphorus pentachloride	10026-13-8	0.1	0.87	-	-	R14, 22, 26, 34, 48/20
Phosphorus trichloride	7719-12-2	0.2	1.1	0.5	2.9	R14, 26/28, 35, 48/20
Phosphorus, yellow	7723-14-0	-	0.1	-	0.3	R11, 16, 52/53
Phosphoryl trichloride	10025-87-3	0.2	1.3	0.6	3.8	R14, 22, 26, 35, 48/23
Phthalic anhydride	85-44-9	-	4	-	12	Sen R22, 37/38, 41, 42/43
Picloram (ISO)	1918-02-1	-	10	-	20	
Picric acid	88-89-1	-	0.1	-	0.3	R2, 4, 23/24/25
Piperazine	110-85-0	-	0.1	-	0.3	Sen R34, 42/43, 52/53
Piperazine dihydrochloride	142-64-3	-	0.1	-	0.3	Sen
Piperidine	110-89-4	1	3.5	-	-	Sk R11, 23/24, 34

Plaster of Paris
  inhalable dust
  respirable dust
	26499-65-0	
		-
		-
			
			10
			4
				
				-
				-
					
					-
					-	

Platinum compds, soluble (except certain halogeno-Pt compounds) (as Pt)		-	0.002	-	-	
Platinum metal	7440-06-4	-	5	-	-	
Polychlorinated biphenyls (PCB)	1336-36-3	-	0.1	-	-	Sk R33, 50/53*

Polyvinyl chloride
  inhalable dust
  respirable dust
	9002-86-2	
		-
		-
			
			10
			4
				
				-
				-
					
					-
					-	

Portland cement
  inhalable dust
  respirable dust
	65997-15-1	
		-
		-
			
			10
			4
				
				-
				-
					
					-
					-	

Potassium hydroxide	1310-58-3	-	-	-	2	R22, 35

Propane-1,2-diol
  total vapour and
  particulates
  particulates
	57-55-6	
		
		150
		-
			
			474
			10
				
				-
				-
					
					-
					-	

Propan-1-ol	71-23-8	200	500	250	625	Sk R11, 41, 67
Propan-2-ol	67-63-0	400	999	500	1250	R11, 36, 67
Propionic acid	79-09-4	10	31	15	46	R34
Propoxur (ISO)	114-26-1	-	0.5	-	2	R25, 50/53
Propranolol	525-66-6	-	2	-	6	
n-Propyl acetate	109-60-4	200	849	250	1060	R11, 36, 66, 67
Propylene oxide	75-56-9	5	12	-	-	Carc R45, 46, 12, 20/21/22, 36/37/38
Prop-2-yn-1-ol	107-19-7	1	2.3	3	7	Sk R10, 23/24/25, 34, 51/53

Pulverised fuel ash
  inhalable dust
  respirable dust
		
		-
		-
			
			10
			4
				
				-
				-
					
					-
					-	

Pyrethrins (ISO)	8003-34-7 121-21-1 121-29-9	-	5	-	10	10 R20/21/22, 50/53
Pyridine	110-86-1	5	16	10	33	R11, 20/21/22

Substance	CAS number	Workplace exposure limit				Comments
		Long-term exposure limit (8-hour TWA reference period)		Short-term exposure limit (15-minute reference period)		
		ppm	mg.m^{-3}	ppm	mg.m^{-3}	
2-Pyridylamine	504-29-0	0.5	2	2	7.8	
Pyrocatechol	120-80-9	5	23	-	-	R21/22, 36/38
Refractory Ceramic Fibres and Special Purpose Fibres		5 mg.m^{-3} 1 fibre/millilitre		-	-	Carc R49, 38
Resorcinol	108-46-3	10	46	20	92	R22, 36/38, 50
Rhodium (as Rh)						
metal fume and dust		-	0.1	-	0.3	
soluble salts		-	0.001	-	0.003	
Rosin-based solder flux fume	8050-09-7	-	0.05	-	0.15	Sen
Rotenone (ISO)	83-79-4	-	5	-	10	R25, 36/37/38, 50/53
Rouge	1309-37-1					
total inhalable		-	10	-	-	
respirable		-	4	-	-	
Rubber fume	See page 30	-	0.6	-	-	Carc Limit relates to cyclohexane soluble material
Rubber process dust	See page 30	-	6	-	-	Carc HSC/E plans to review the limit values for this substance
Selenium and compounds, except hydrogen selenide (as Se)		-	0.1	-	-	
Silane	7803-62-5	0.5	0.67	1	1.3	
Silica, amorphous						
inhalable dust		-	6	-	-	
respirable dust		-	2.4	-	-	
Silica, respirable crystalline	see page 31	-	0.3	-	-	HSC/E plans to review the limit values for this substance
Silica, fused respirable dust	60676-86-0	-	0.08	-	-	
Silicon	7440-21-3					
inhalable dust		-	10	-	-	
respirable dust		-	4	-	-	
Silicon carbide (not whiskers)	409-21-2					
total inhalable		-	10	-	-	
respirable		-	4	-	-	
Silver (soluble compounds as Ag)		-	0.01	-	-	
Silver, metallic	7440-22-4	-	0.1	-	-	
Sodium azide (as NaN$_3$)	26628-22-8	-	0.1	-	0.3	Sk R28, 32, 50/53

Substance	CAS number	Workplace exposure limit				Comments
		Long-term exposure limit (8-hour TWA reference period)		Short-term exposure limit (15-minute reference period)		
		ppm	mg.m^{-3}	ppm	mg.m^{-3}	
Sodium 2-(2,4-dichlorophenoxy) ethyl sulphate	136-78-7	-	10	-	20	
Sodium hydrogen sulphite	7631-90-5	-	5	-	-	R22, 31
Sodium hydroxide	1310-73-2	-	-	-	2	R35
Softwood dust	See page 31	-	5	-	-	Sen HSC/E plans to review the limit values for this substance

Starch
  total inhalable
  respirable
	9005-25-8	-
		-
			10
			4
				-
				-
					-
					-	

Styrene	100-42-5	100	430	250	1080	R10, 20, 36/38 HSC/E plans to review the limit values for this substance
Subtilisins	1395-21-7 (*Bacillus subtilis* BPN) 9014-01-1 (*Bacillus subtilis* Carlsberg)	-	0.00004	-	-	Sen R37/38, 41, 42
Sucrose	57-50-1	-	10	-	20	
Sulfotep (ISO)	3689-24-5	-	0.1	-	-	Sk R27/28, 50/53*
Sulphur hexafluoride	2551-62-4	1000	6070	1250	7590	
Sulphuryl difluoride	2699-79-8	5	21	10	42	R23, 48/20, 50*
o-Toluidine	95-53-4	0.2	0.89	-	-	Carc Sk R45, 23/25, 36, 50
Talc, respirable dust	14807-96-6	-	1	-	-	
Tantalum	7440-25-7	-	5	-	10	
Tellurium & compounds, except hydrogen telluride, (as Te)		-	0.1	-	-	
Terphenyls, all isomers	26140-60-3	-	-	0.5	4.8	
1,1,2,2-Tetrabromoethane	79-27-6	0.5	7.2	-	-	Sk R26, 36, 52/53*
Tetracarbonylnickel	13463-39-3	-	-	0.1	0.24	R11, 26, 40, 61, 50/53
Tetrachloroethylene	127-18-4	50	345	100	689	R40, 50/53
1,1,1,2-Tetrafluoroethane (HFC 134a)	811-97-2	1000	4240	-	-	
Tetrahydrofuran	109-99-9	50	150	100	300	Sk R11, 19, 36/37
Tetrasodium pyrophosphate	7722-88-5	-	5	-	-	
Thallium, soluble compounds (as Tl)		-	0.1	-	-	Sk
Thionyl chloride	7719-09-7	-	-	1	4.9	R14, 20/22, 29, 35

Substance	CAS number	Workplace exposure limit				Comments
		Long-term exposure limit (8-hour TWA reference period) ppm	mg.m^{-3}	Short-term exposure limit (15-minute reference period) ppm	mg.m^{-3}	
Tin compounds, inorganic, except SnH$_4$, (as Sn)		-	2	-	4	
Tin compounds, organic, except Cyhexatin (ISO), (as Sn)		-	0.1	-	0.2	Sk
Titanium dioxide	13463-67-7					
total inhalable		-	10	-	-	
respirable		-	4	-	-	
Toluene	108-88-3	50	191	150	574	Sk R11, 38, 48/20, 63, 65, 67*
p-Toluenesulphonyl chloride	98-59-9	-	-	-	5	
Tributyl phosphate, all isomers	126-73-8	-	5	-	5	R22, 38, 40*
1,2,4-Trichlorobenzene	120-82-1	1	-	5	-	Sk R22, 38, 50/53
1,1,1-Trichloroethane	71-55-6	100	555	200	1110	R20, 59
Trichloroethylene	79-01-6	100	550	150	820	Carc, Sk R45, 36/38, 67, 52/53 HSC/E plans to review the limit values for this substance
Trichloronitromethane	76-06-2	0.1	0.68	0.3	2.1	R22, 26, 36/37/38
Triethylamine	121-44-8	2	8	4	17	Sk R11, 20/21/22, 35
Triglycidyl isocyanurate (TGIC)	2451-62-9	-	0.1	-	-	Carc R46, 23/25, 41, 43, 48/22, 52/53
Trimellitic anhydride	552-30-7	-	0.04	-	0.12	Sen R37, 41, 42/43
Trimethylbenzenes, all isomers or mixtures	25551-13-7	25	125	-	-	
3,5,5-trimethylcyclohex-2-enone	78-59-1	-	-	5	29	R21/22, 36/37, 40
Trimethyl phosphite	121-45-9	2	10	-	-	
2,4,6-Trinitrotoluene	118-96-7	-	0.5	-	-	Sk R2, 23/24/25, 33, 51/53
Tri-o-tolyl phosphate	78-30-8	-	0.1	-	0.3	R39/23/24/25, 51/53
Triphenyl phosphate	115-86-6	-	3	-	6	
Tungsten & compounds (as W)	7440-33-7					
soluble compounds		-	1	-	3	
insoluble compounds and others		-	5	-	10	
Turpentine	8006-64-2	100	566	150	850	R10, 20/21/22, 36/38, 43, 65, 51/53
Vanadium pentoxide	1314-62-1	-	0.05	-	-	R20/22, 37, 48/23, 63, 68, 51/53
Vinyl chloride	75-01-4	3	-	-	-	Carc R45, 12

Substance	CAS number	Workplace exposure limit				Comments
		Long-term exposure limit (8-hour TWA reference period)		Short-term exposure limit (15-minute reference period)		
		ppm	mg.m^{-3}	ppm	mg.m^{-3}	
Vinylidene chloride	75-35-4	10	40	-	-	R12, 20, 40*
Wool process dust	See page 31	-	10	-	-	
Xylene, o-,m-,p- or mixed isomers	1330-20-7	50	220	100	441	Sk BMGV R10, 20/21, 38
Yttrium	7440-65-5	-	1	-	3	
Zinc chloride, fume	7646-85-7	-	1	-	2	R22, 34, 50/53*
Zinc distearate	557-05-1					
inhalable dust		-	10	-	20	
respirable dust		-	4	-	-	
Zirconium compounds (as Zr)		-	5	-	10	

Table 2: Biological Monitoring Guidance Values

17   The framework for the use of biological monitoring and the setting of Biological Monitoring Guidance Values (BMGVs) is detailed in paragraphs 114-116. For each substance with a BMGV a free information sheet briefly describing a suggested analytical method, appropriate sampling strategy, the availability of quality assurance schemes and interpretation of results is available. Information sheets can be obtained from HSE's Health and Safety Laboratory, Biomedical Sciences Group, Health & Safety Laboratory, Health Sciences (or Biological Monitoring), Buxton, Derbyshire, SK17 9JN (Website: www.hsl.gov.uk).

Substance	Biological Monitoring Guidance Value	Sampling time
Butan-2-one	70 µmol butan-2-one/L in urine	Post shift
2-Butoxyethanol	240 mmol butoxyacetic acid/mol creatinine in urine	Post shift
Carbon monoxide	30 ppm carbon monoxide in end-tidal breath	Post shift
Chromium VI	10 µmol chromium/mol creatinine in urine	Post shift
Cyclohexanone	2 mmol cyclohexanol/mol creatinine in urine	Post shift
Dichloromethane	30 ppm carbon monoxide in end-tidal breath	Post shift
N,N-Dimethylacetamide	100 mmol N-methylacetamide/mol creatinine in urine	Post shift
Glycerol trinitrate (Nitroglycerin)	15 µmol total nitroglycols/mol creatinine in urine	At the end of the period of exposure
Lindane (γBHC(ISO))	35 nmol/L (10 µg/L) of lindane in whole blood (equivalent to 70 nmol/L of lindane in plasma)	Random
MbOCA (2,2' dichloro-4,4' methylene dianiline)	15 µmol total MbOCA/mol creatinine in urine	Post shift
Mercury	20 µmol mercury/mol creatinine in urine	Random
4-methylpentan-2-one	20 µmol 4-methylpentan-2-one/L in urine	Post shift
4,4'-Methylenedianimile (MDA)	50 µmol total MDA/mol creatinine in urine	Post shift for inhalation and pre-shift next day for dermal exposure
Polycyclic aromatic hydrocarbons (PAHs)	4 µmol 1-hydroxypyrene/mol creatinine in urine	Post shift
Xylene, o-, m-, p- or mixed isomers	650 mmol methyl hippuric acid/mol creatinine in urine	Post shift

Supplementary information for Table 1

Definitions

Cotton dust

18   Cotton is the cellulose fibre that grows inside the seed pods (or bolls) of the cotton plant. When mature, the boll breaks and the cotton appears as a soft wad of fine fibres. After picking, the cotton is separated from the seed etc, and is packed and compressed into bales.

19   The WEL, which is based on personal sampling, applies to exposure to inhalable dust during the handling of raw and waste cotton including blends containing raw or waste cotton, with the following exceptions:

(a)   dust from weaving, knitting, braiding and subsequent processes;

(b)   dust from bleached or dyed cotton; and

(c)   dust from finished articles, for example garments.

(Where the WEL does not apply, exposure should still be adequately controlled.)

20   MDHS14/3 *General methods for sampling and gravimetric analysis of respirable and inhalable dust*[13] gives information about air sampling for comparison with the WEL. The sampler should be an IOM inhalable dust sampler or any other sampler giving equivalent results.

Ferrous foundry particulate

21   The atmospheric contamination in ferrous (iron and steel) foundries is a complex mixture of dust, fume, gases and vapours produced as a consequence of the foundry processes. The particulate fraction of the atmospheric contamination is described as ferrous foundry particulate (FFP). The composition of FFP will vary according to the process producing it and the materials used.

22   During the making of cores and moulds, vapours and gases from the binder system may be given off, and particles of sand, including respirable silica (possibly coated with unreacted or reacted binder materials) can become airborne. When molten metal is poured into the moulds, decomposition products can be produced from organic binders and additives in the mould. The decomposition products may bind to particles of sand or metal oxide. At knockout and shakeout, sand particles (which may be coated with thermally degraded binder material) are the main contaminants produced. Metal finishing operations can give rise to fume as well as airborne metal, metal oxide particles and coated sand particles.

23   Some of the individual components of the atmospheric contamination are known to be carcinogenic or mutagenic and some have been assigned WELs. The interrelationship between the components of FFP is complex and it is inappropriate to rely on the individual WELs in assessing overall exposure to airborne contaminants in the foundry atmosphere.

Airborne particulate is considered to be a suitable surrogate for overall exposure assessment in ferrous foundries. FFP is measured as total inhalable particulate (TIP) and respirable particulate (RP). Where identified components of the contamination have WELs these limits will apply.

Flour dust

24   Flour dust is taken to be finely ground particles of cereals or pulses (including contaminants) that result from any grinding process and from any subsequent handling and use of that 'flour'. Any additives (eg flour improvers) are included in this definition only after they have been added to the final product mix.

Grain dust

25   Grain dust is taken to be dust arising from the harvesting, drying, handling, storage or processing of barley, wheat, oats, maize and rye, including contaminants.

Halogeno-platinum compounds

26   These are co-ordination compounds in which a platinum atom or ion is directly co-ordinated to one or more halide (ie fluoride, chloride, bromide or iodide) ions. These compounds are subject to a WEL and have a Sen notation. These substances are listed in section C of *Asthmagen? Critical assessments of the evidence for agents implicated in occupational asthma.*[4]

27   For substances which, although they contain platinum and halide ions, the halogen is not directly co-coordinated by a chemical bond to the platinum, the WEL for soluble platinum compounds is applicable.

Machine-made mineral fibres (MMMF)

28   Machine-made (formerly 'man-made') mineral fibres are defined as man-made vitreous (silicate) fibres with random orientation with alkaline oxide and alkali earth oxide ($Na_2O+K_2O+CaO+MgO+BaO$) content greater than 18% by weight. Neither the gravimetric limit nor the fibres in air limits should be exceeded. Fibre concentrations of MMMFs must be measured or calculated by a method approved by HSC.

29   A separate limit applies to other MMMFs which are not covered by this definition (see paragraph 31).

Pulverised fuel ash

30   Pulverised fuel ash (PFA), sometimes known as precipitation ash, is a fine grey fuel ash powder, composed mainly of alumino-silicate amorphous spheres. It is produced when pulverised coal is burnt in a coal-fired power station. It is collected and separated into various grades for use as a filler in civil engineering and land reclamation, in ready-mix concrete, as a grout in block/cementitious products and in the manufacture of other products used by the construction industry.

Refractory ceramic fibre (RCF)

31   RCFs are man-made vitreous (silicate) fibres with random orientation with alkaline oxide and alkali earth oxide ($Na_2O+K_2O+CaO+MgO+BaO$) content less or equal to 18% by weight. The term 'RCF' also includes non-oxide ceramic fibre such as boron and silicon carbides and nitrides. Fibre concentrations of RCF must be measured or calculated by a method approved by the HSC.

Rubber fume and rubber process dust

32   Rubber fume is fume evolved in the mixing, milling and blending of natural rubber or synthetic elastomers, or of natural rubber and synthetic polymers combined with chemicals, and in the processes which convert the resultant blends into finished process dust products or parts thereof, and including any inspection procedures where fume continues to be evolved.

33   The limit relates to cyclohexane soluble material determined by the method described in MDHS47/2 *Determination of rubber process dust and rubber fume in air.*[14]

34   Rubber process dust is dust arising in the stages of rubber manufacture where ingredients are handled, weighed, added to or mixed with uncured material or synthetic elastomers. It does not include dusts arising from the abrasion of cured rubber.

35   Where the airborne material contains a mixture of substances, one or more of which is assigned a WEL, that limit will apply to the individual substance and at the same time the rubber process dust limit will apply to the mix dust as a whole. Where the airborne material is effectively a single substance with a WEL, that limit alone will apply.

36   Methods for personal sampling and measurement of inhalable dusts are available in MDHS14/3: *General methods for sampling and gravimetric analysis of respirable and inhalable dust*[13] and MDHS47/2: *Determination of rubber process dust and rubber fume in air.*[14] As with the fume, the dust is determined gravimetrically but, unlike the fume, the dust determination does not involve solvent extraction.

Note: Dust produced by the abrasion of cured rubber should be dealt with as described in paragraphs 42-45, ie dust of any kind when present at a substantial concentration in air is covered by COSHH.

Subtilisins

37 Subtilisins are proteolytic enzymes derived from *Bacillus subtilis*.They are used in biological washing powders, animal feedstuffs etc. The enzyme preparation contains active enzyme, inactive enzyme and protein residues. The WEL for subtilisins is 0.00004 mg.m^{-3} (8-hr TWA) - 40 ng.m^{-3} - crystalline active pure enzyme. One of the suitable measurement methods is the fluorescence polarisation technique developed by the Health and Safety Laboratory (HSL). The previous limit for subtilisin was based on high-volume static sampling to achieve sufficient sensitivity. However, improvements in the analytical methodology have improved the sensitivity and the WEL for subtilisin reflects this. The limit is based on standard personal sampling (MDHS14/3).[13] Short-term reference period (15 minute) sampling is not appropriate.

Talc

38 Talc is defined as the mineral talc together with other hydrous phyllosilicates including chlorite and carbonate materials which occur with it, but excluding amphibole asbestos and crystalline silica.

Wood dust

39 Wood dust is a general term covering a wide variety of airborne wood dusts. Timbers have been divided into two different groups, namely hardwoods and softwoods. Hardwoods are timbers from deciduous trees, including trees from both temperate and tropical zones, such as beech, ash, oak, mahogany and teak. Softwoods are mainly from coniferous trees such as Scots pine, yew and cedar.

40 Dust is generated by the machining and working of wood and wood-containing materials such as chipboard and fibreboard. Operations such as sawing, turning and routing produce relatively coarse dust, while sanding and assembly operations generate fine dust.

Wool process dust

41 Wool process dust is the term used to describe the dust generated in the production of woollen and worsted textiles. This includes all factory processes from the receipt of the raw wool up to the finished product in the case of carpet manufacture, and up to, and including, weaving, knitting or non-woven cloth production. It does not cover agricultural processes, including any sorting or baling done on the farm. The term 'wool', in this case, refers to sheep's wool and wool blends only. It does not include other speciality fibres - such as goat hair (including cashmere and mohair), camel hair or alpaca. Such fibres differ from wool in structure and it is not certain that the composition of the dust or the potential health risk is the same as with wool process dust.

Dust

42 The COSHH definition of a substance hazardous to health includes dust of any kind when present at a concentration in air equal to or greater than 10 mg.m^{-3} 8-hour TWA of inhalable dust or 4 mg.m^{-3} 8-hour TWA of respirable dust. This means that any dust will be subject to COSHH if people are exposed above these levels. Advice on control is given in EH44 *Dust: General principles of protection*[15] and in the great majority of workplaces reasonable control measures will normally keep exposure below these levels. However, some dusts have been assigned specific WELs and exposure to these must comply with the appropriate limit.

43 Most industrial dusts contain particles of a wide range of sizes. The behaviour, deposition and fate of any particular particle after entry into the human respiratory system and the body response that it elicits, depend on the nature and size of the particle. HSE distinguishes two size fractions for limit-setting purposes termed 'inhalable' and 'respirable'.

44 Inhalable dust approximates to the fraction of airborne material that enters the nose and mouth during breathing and is therefore available for deposition in the respiratory tract. **Respirable dust** approximates to the fraction that penetrates to the gas exchange region of the lung. Fuller definitions and explanatory material are given in MDHS14/3 *General methods for sampling and gravimetric analysis of respirable and inhalable dust.*[13]

45 Where dusts contain components that have their own assigned workplace exposure limits, all the relevant limits should be complied with.

Fume

46 The word 'fume' is often used to include gases and vapours. This is not the case for exposure limits where 'fume' should normally be applied to solid particles generated by chemical reactions or condensed from the gaseous state, usually after volatilisation from melted substances. The generation of fume is often accompanied by a chemical reaction such as oxidation or thermal breakdown.

Substances which are special cases under COSHH or other legislation

Carcinogenic and mutagenic substances

47 Regulation 7(5) of COSHH sets out clear requirements for the control of carcinogenic and mutagenic substances. Appendix 1 of the COSHH (ACOP) gives additional practical guidance. The ACOP applies to any carcinogenic or mutagen defined as such in COSHH. This will include:

(a) any substance or preparation which if classified in

accordance with regulation 5 of the Chemicals (Hazard Information and Packaging for Supply) Regulations would be in the category of danger, carcinogenic (category 1) or carcinogenic (category 2), or mutagenic (category 1) or mutagenic (category 2) whether or not the substance or preparation would be required to be classified under those regulations; or

(b)   any substance or preparation listed in Schedule 1 and any substances or preparation arising from a process specified in Schedule 1 which is a substance hazardous to health.

This definition also covers substances and preparations which would require labelling with the risk phrases 'R45', 'R46' or 'R49' if they were not exceptions to all or part of the Chemicals (Hazard Information and Packaging for Supply) Regulations. Examples of these exceptions are medicines, unpackaged substances and substances being moved around within a factory.

48   The substances, preparations and processes defined as carcinogens or mutagens for the purpose of the COSHH Regulations and to which the special provisions for carcinogens and mutagens in the COSHH Regulations apply are listed in the *Approved Supply List*[12] and the COSHH ACOP.[5]

49   A list of the other substances and processes to which the definition of 'carcinogen' relates is given below:

(a)   aflatoxins;

(b)   arsenic;

(c)   auramine manufacture;

(d)   calcining, sintering or smelting of nickel copper matte or acid leaching or electrorefining of roasted matte;

(e)   coal soots, coal tar, pitch and coal tar fumes;

(f)   hardwood dusts;

(g)   isopropyl alcohol manufacture (strong acid process);

(h)   leather dust in boot and shoe manufacture, arising during preparation and finishing;

(i)   magenta manufacture;

(j)   mustard gas (β,β'-dichlorodiethyl sulphide);

(k)   rubber manufacturing and processing giving rise to rubber process dust and rubber fume;

(l)   used engine oils;

(m)   the following polychlorodibenzodioxins:
(i)   2,3,7,8-TCDD,
(ii)   1,2,3,7,8-PeCDD,
(iii)   1,2,3,4,7,8-HxCDD,
(iv)   1,2,3,6,7,8-HxCDD,
(v)   1,2,3,7,8,9 -HxCDD,
(vi)   1,2,3,4,6,7,8-HpCDD,
(vii)   OCDD;

(n)   the following polychlorodibenzofurans:
(i)   2,3,7,8-TCDF,
(ii)   2,3,4,7,8-PeCDF,
(iii)   1,2,3,7,8-PeCDF,
(iv)   1,2,3,4,7,8-HxCDF,
(v)   1,2,3,7,8,9-HxCDF,
(vi)   1,2,3,6,7,8-HxCDF,
(vii)   2,3,4,6,7,8-HxCDF,
(viii)   1,2,3,4,6,7,8-HpCDF,
(viiii)   1,2,3,4,7,8,9-HpCDF,
(x)   OCDF,

where T=tetra, Pe=penta, Hx=hexa, Hp=hepta and O=Octa.

Asbestos

50   Exposure to asbestos must be prevented or, where that is not reasonably practicable, it must be reduced to the lowest level that is reasonably practicable.

51   The Control of Asbestos at Work Regulations[17] set control limits for asbestos based on both 4-hour and 10 minute TWAs. They also set action levels based on cumulative exposure which determine whether or not certain regulations apply in any given case. HSC has approved a method of measurement which must be used when fibre levels are being checked against any of these limits.

52   Information about the exposure limits and measurement methods for asbestos is given in *Asbestos: The analysts' guide for sampling, analysis and clearance procedures*[18] which also contains guidance on the use of airborne fibre measurement in checking the effectiveness of enclosures or other control measures, or for site clearance when work is finished. More technical detail about measurement is also given in this publication.

53   For more information see the control of Asbestos at Work Regulations and supporting ACOPS.[19-22]

Control limits and action levels
54   The control limits to be used depend upon the type of asbestos which is present. The limits are more stringent when amphibole asbestos (eg amosite or crocidolite) are present, either alone or as mixtures of amphiboles or amphiboles with chrystotile. For each of the two categories (with and without amphibole asbestos) there are two limits:

one is a limit on the average fibre level over any continuous 4-hour period, and the other is a limit on the average fibre level over any continuous 10-minute period. Each is a control limit in its own right. If either is exceeded, then suitable RPE is required under regulation 8, and respirator zones must be designated, under regulation 14 of the Control of Asbestos at Work Regulations.[17]

55   The control limits as defined in the Regulations are:

(a)   for chrysotile:
   (i)   0.3 fibres per millilitre of air averaged over any continuous period of 4 hours;
   (ii)   0.9 fibres per millilitre of air averaged over any continuous period of 10 minutes;

(b)   for any other form of asbestos either alone or in mixtures including mixtures of chrysotile with any other form of asbestos:

   (i)   0.2 fibres per millilitre of air averaged over any continuous period of 4 hours;
   (ii)   0.6 fibres per millilitre of air averaged over any continuous period of 10 minutes.

Employers may choose to assume that the asbestos is not chrysotile alone and apply the more stringent limits; they do not then need to identify the type of asbestos.

56   The action levels apply to exposure in the longer term. They are specified as cumulative exposures within any continuous 12-week period. Cumulative exposure is calculated by multiplying each airborne fibre level by the time for which it lasts and adding up all these products over the 12-week period in question. If the exposure of any employee exceeds an action level, then the regulations on notification, designated areas and medical surveillance apply (regulations 6,14 and 16 respectively).

57   The action levels are:

(a)   where the exposure is solely to chrysotile, 72 fibre-hours per millilitre of air; or

(b)   where the exposure is to any other form of asbestos whether alone or in mixtures including mixtures of chryostile with any other form of asbestos, 48 fibre-hours per millilitre of air; or

(c)   where both types of exposure occur separately during the 12-week period concerned, a proportionate number of fibre-hours per millilitre of air.

58   The composite limit at (c) above applies only when the two types of exposure occur at different times within the 12-week period; if both types of asbestos are present simultaneously the mixture must be treated as if it were not chrysotile alone.

Lead

The occupational exposure limits for lead
59   The occupational exposure limits for lead are set out in the Control of Lead at Work Regulations 2002 (CLAW).[23]

60   The limits are 8-hour TWA concentrations as follows:

(a)   in relation to lead other than lead alkyls, a concentration of lead in the atmosphere to which any employee is exposed of 0.15 mg.m^{-3}; and

(b)   in relation to lead alkyls, a concentration of lead in the atmosphere to which any employee is exposed of 0.10mg.m^{-3}.

When determining lead-in-air concentrations for comparison with the occupational exposure limits, the method referred to in regulation 9 of CLAW and described in *Control of lead at work. Control of Lead at Work Regulations 2002. Approved Code of Practice and guidance* [24] should be used.

61   Unlike the former lead-in-air standards which could be exceeded in certain specified circumstances, the exposure limits for lead are ceiling limits which must not be exceeded when calculated as time-weighted averages over 8 hours.

62   As far as exposure by inhalation is concerned, control is considered adequate when exposure does not exceed the appropriate exposure limit. It should be remembered that other routes of exposure to lead are also important, eg ingestion, or contact with the skin where there is exposure to lead alkyls.

The biological limits for lead
63   The CLAW Regulations also contain biological limits as additional measures designed to control employees' exposure to lead. For employees exposed to inorganic lead, the limits are based on the concentration of lead in the blood and expressed as micrograms of lead per decilitre of blood (μg/dl). For employees exposed to lead alkyls, the limits are based on the concentration of lead in urine and the values expressed in units of μg Pb/g creatinine.

Action levels:

64   Where the blood-lead concentration for any employee reaches or exceeds the action level, the employer has a statutory duty to determine why and, so far as is reasonably practicable, to take steps to reduce the employee's blood-lead to below the action level. The action levels are:

(a)   in respect of a woman of reproductive capacity, 25 μg/dl;

(b)   in respect of a young person (aged under 18), 40 μg/dl;

(c)   in respect of any other employee, 50 μg/dl.

There are no action levels for work involving exposure to lead alkyls.

65   The purpose of the action level is to give the employer early warning that an employee's blood-level concentration is approaching the suspension level so that steps can be taken to prevent it being triggered.

Suspension levels:

66   When the blood-lead (for employees exposed to inorganic lead) or urinary lead (for employees exposed to lead alkyls) concentration of any employee reaches or exceeds the suspension level, the employer will normally remove the employee from work involving further exposure to lead in order to protect the employee's health. The suspension levels are:

(a)   a blood-level concentration of:
  (i)   in respect of a woman of reproductive capacity, 30 µg/dl;
  (ii)   in respect of a young person (aged under 18), 50 µg/dl;
  (iii) in respect of any other employee, 60 µg/dl; or

(b)   urinary lead concentration of:
  (i)   in respect of a woman of reproductive capacity, 25 µg Pb/g creatinine (14 µmol/mol creatinine);
  (ii)   in respect of any other employee, 110 µg Pb/g creatinine (55 µmol/mol creatinine).

67   The employer will only allow the employee to resume work involving exposure to lead when the doctor responsible for carrying out medical surveillance on the employee concerned confirms that the employee's blood or urinary lead concentration has dropped back below the suspension levels.

Substances that can cause occupational asthma

68   Substances that can cause occupational asthma (also known as asthmagens and respiratory sensitisers) can induce a state of specific airway hyper-responsiveness via an immunological, irritant or other mechanism. Once the airways have become hyper-responsive, further exposure to the substance, sometimes even to tiny quantities, may cause respiratory symptoms. These symptoms can range in severity from a runny nose to asthma. Not all workers who are exposed to a sensitiser will become hyper-responsive and it is impossible to identify in advance those who are likely to become hyper-responsive. Substances that can cause occupational asthma are classified under the *Chemicals (Hazard Information and Packaging for Supply) Regulations (CHIP)*[16] and assigned the risk phrase 'R42 May cause sensitisation by inhalation' or 'R42/43 May cause sensitisation by inhalation and skin contact' in the *Approved supply list*.[12]

69   Substances that can cause occupational asthma should be distinguished from substances which may trigger the symptoms of asthma in people with pre-existing airway hyper-responsiveness, but which do not include the disease themselves. The latter substances are not classified asthmagens or respiratory sensitisers.

70   Wherever it is reasonably practicable, exposure to substances that can cause occupational asthma should be prevented. Where this is not possible, the primary aim is to apply adequate standards of control to prevent workers from becoming hyper-responsive. For substances that can cause occupational asthma, COSHH requires that exposure be reduced as low as is reasonably practicable. Activities giving rise to short-term peak concentrations should receive particular attention when risk management is being considered. Health surveillance is appropriate for all employees exposed or liable to be exposed to a substance which may cause occupational asthma and there should be appropriate consultation with an occupational health professional over the degree of risk and level of surveillance.

71   The 'Sen' notation in the list of WELs has been assigned only to those substances which may cause occupational asthma in the categories shown in Table 1 (see page 5). It should be remembered that other substances not in these tables may cause occupational asthma.

72   HSE's asthma web pages (http://www.hse.gov.uk/asthma) provide information about:

(a)   the main causes of occupational asthma;
(b)   what it is like to get the disease;
(c)   what employers have to do to protect their employees; and
(d)   what HSE and stakeholders are doing to tackle the problem.

73   A number of HSE publications provide additional advice on substances which may cause occupational asthma and their control in the workplace. *Preventing asthma at work: How to control respiratory sensitisers*[25] provides step-by-step advice on strategies which can be adopted for preventing or adequately controlling exposure to these asthmagens. *Asthmagen? Critical assessments of the evidence for agents implicated in occupational asthma*[4] includes substances which, on the balance of evidence, should not be considered to be asthmagens as well as those that should. Further information on health surveillance can be found in MS25 *Medical aspects of occupational asthma.*[26]

Asphyxiants

74   Some gases and vapours, when present at high concentrations in air, act as simple asphyxiants by reducing the oxygen content by dilution to such an extent that life cannot be supported. Many asphyxiants are odourless and

colourless and not readily detectable. Monitoring the oxygen content of the air is often the best means of ensuring safety. There are substantial risks if the concentration of oxygen in the atmosphere varies from normal (20.8%) under normal atmospheric pressure. With reference to specific statutory requirements, any difference in oxygen content from normal should be investigated, the risks assessed, and appropriate measures taken in the light of the risk. In particular, the *Mines and Quarries Act 1954*[27] (Section 55) refer to the duty upon the manager of every mine to secure ventilation below ground adequate for diluting gases and providing air containing sufficient oxygen. Section 55(2)(b) specifies the amount of oxygen in the general body of the air as not less than 19% by volume.

75   Particular care is necessary when dense asphyxiants, eg argon, are used since localised very high concentrations can arise due to their collecting in pits, confined spaces and other low-lying areas where ventilation is likely to be poor.

76   Many asphyxiants present a fire or explosion risk. The concentrations at which these risks can arise are liable to be well below those at which asphyxiation is likely to occur and should be taken into account when assessing the hazards.

Pesticides

77   Substances used as active ingredients in pesticides are listed under their systematic chemical names and/or their (ISO) common names. These may sometimes be used as parts of the names of proprietary pesticide formulations. In all cases the exposure limit applies to the specific active ingredient in the workplace atmosphere and not the formulation as a whole.

Exposure in mines

78   The control of dust below ground in coal mines is covered by section 74 of the *Mines and Quarries Act 1954*[27] which requires the manager of a coal mine to minimise the 'giving off' of injurious dust below ground and the *Coal Mines (Respirable Dust) Regulations 1975*[28] which cover the respirable fraction of total inhalable dust.

79   By Autumn 2005, a new set of regulations, are expected to be introduced to govern the control of inhalable dust below ground in coal mines. The *Coal Mines (Control of Inhalable Dust) Regulations*, will be announced on the HSE website.

EH40/2005 Workplace exposure limits

Setting exposure limits

Legal background to exposure limits

80   HSC has established WELs for a number of substances hazardous to health. These are intended to prevent excessive exposure to specified hazardous substances by containing exposure below a set limit. A WEL is the maximum concentration of an airborne substance averaged over a reference period, to which employees may be exposed by inhalation.

Approach to deriving the workplace exposure limit

81   The first stage in the derivation of the WEL involves an assessment of the toxicology of the substance concerned. The purpose of this assessment is to identify the potential for a substance to produce adverse human health effects and to understand the exposure-response relationships for these effects. In the context of OEL-setting, there are certain key reference points on the exposure-response curve. These are the 'No-Observed Adverse Effect Level' (NOAEL) and the 'Lowest-Observed Adverse Effect Level' (LOAEL). The concept of NOAELs/LOAELs is generally agreed to have practical relevance in the OEL-setting context only for those substances or toxicological mechanisms that have a 'threshold' of effect. For example, eye irritation caused by an acid vapour will only occur above a certain threshold exposure concentration, and thus the concept of a NOAEL will apply. In contrast, for substances such as DNA-reactive chemicals that cause cancer by a genotoxic mechanism, although in theory a threshold may exist, (because of biochemical defence and repair mechanisms) currently available techniques do not allow the reliable identification of a clear threshold or NOAEL. (The NOAEL is the highest point on the exposure-response curve at which no adverse health effects are observed; the LOAEL is the lowest point on the exposure-response curve at which adverse health effects are observed).

82   If a NOAEL (or LOAEL) can be identified, then this value is taken as a starting point for estimating the highest level of occupational exposure at which no adverse health effects would be expected to occur in workers or their progeny following exposure over a working lifetime. Given that in many cases, NOAELs/LOAELs are obtained from studies in animals, numerical 'uncertainty factors' (sometimes referred to as 'safety factors') are usually applied in order to arrive at this estimated desired level of exposure. These factors are applied to take account of toxicological uncertainties such as possible species differences in response, and also to take account of human variability in responsiveness.

83   An across-government initiative has examined the ways in which different government departments and agencies deal with toxicological uncertainty in risk assessment and standard-setting procedures.[29] The results of this work can be accessed at http://www.le.ac.uk/ieh/pdf/cr9.pdf. In the light of this information ACTS and its scientific subcommittee may develop a more formalised approach on the use of uncertainty factors for setting WELs.

84   Having determined the highest level of occupational exposure at which no adverse health effects would be predicted to occur, the next stage is to determine whether this level of exposure is currently being achieved in the workplace. If not, then consideration would be given to the potential for improving existing standards of control such that this level of

exposure could be reasonably achieved. If ACTS consider this level of exposure is reasonably practicable, then the WEL will be proposed at this level.

85   This route to deriving the WEL will result in a limit set at a level at which no adverse health effects would be expected to occur in workers or their progeny, based on the known and/or predicted effects of the substance, and would also be reasonably practicable for industry to achieve.

86   There are some categories of substance for which this route to deriving a WEL, based on the concept of a NOAEL/LOAEL will not be possible:

(a)   Genotoxic carcinogens: For such substances, there are no currently available techniques by which it is generally accepted that a NOAEL can be reliably identified; hence an approach based on a NOAEL cannot be applied.

(b)   Asthmagens: although the concept of a NOAEL may be valid, the quality of the available data means that it is generally not possible to identify a threshold level of occupational exposure below which there would be no risk of developing the disease;

(c)   Mixtures of variable composition such as metalworking fluids (MWFs): The variable composition means that MWFs pose a variable hazard. A defined position on the likely human health effects and the identification of single NOAEL value is not possible;

(d)   Any other substance for which the balance of doubt and uncertainty about likely human health effects is such that a NOAEL or threshold for effect cannot be confidently identified or predicted. This is more likely to apply to substances with inadequate toxicity data-sets. What is meant by an 'adequate data-set', particularly in the context of OEL-setting, is difficult to define, as it varies according to the nature of the substance, and other factors such as the ability to 'read-across' to data-sets on similar substances. Expert judgement on a case-by-case basis will be needed to determine whether a particular data-set is adequate to predict health effects confidently;

(e)   For some substances, a NOAEL/LOAEL may be identifiable from which it is possible to estimate a level of exposure at which no adverse human health effects would be predicted to occur. However, after due consideration of the costs and efficacy of available control solutions, ACTS may consider that it would not be reasonably practical to control below this desired level of exposure across all industry sectors.

87   For substances belonging in one of the above categories (a)-(e), the WEL would be derived by identifying a level of exposure which would represent a standard of control commensurate with good occupational hygiene

practice. In determining this level, the severity of the likely health effects, and the cost and efficacy of control solutions would have to be taken into account. Agreement on what represents a good standard of control will be for ACTS and its scientific subcommittee, informed by:

(a)   knowledge of the standards of control currently being achieved in different industry sectors using the substance;

(b)   the potential for improving standards; and

(c)   the potential health impact of the substance.

88   For example, a good standard of control for a non-reactive dust such as titanium dioxide would not be considered adequate for a cytotoxic dust such as cyclophosphamide. For substances that have had little or no safety testing, for which the potential health hazards are highly uncertain, good practice would dictate the need for an increased stringency of control as a precautionary measure. The process of deriving the value of the WEL would be an iterative one, involving comparisons of the costs of achieving successively lower proposed WEL values against the estimated health benefits until agreement on an appropriate value is reached. The arguments and rationale for each substance would be set out in Regulatory Impact Assessment documents. In relation to this proposed route to OEL-setting, as far as possible, the WEL would **not** be set at a level at which there is positive evidence of adverse effects on human health.

89   A diagrammatic summary of the proposed OEL-setting process is presented as Figure 1 (page 39).

Criteria for setting workplace exposure limits

90   WELs are derived by the following criteria:

(a)   the WEL value would be set at a level at which no adverse effects on human health would be expected to occur based on the known and/or predicted effects of the substance. However, if such a level cannot be identified with reasonable confidence (categories (a)-(d) in paragraph 86), or if this level is not reasonably achievable (category (e) in paragraph 86); then,

(b)   the WEL value would be based at a level corresponding to what is considered to represent good control, taking into account the severity of the likely health hazards and the costs and efficacy of control solutions. Wherever possible, the WEL would not be set at a level at which there is evidence of adverse effects on human health.

Figure 1 Summary of WEL-setting process

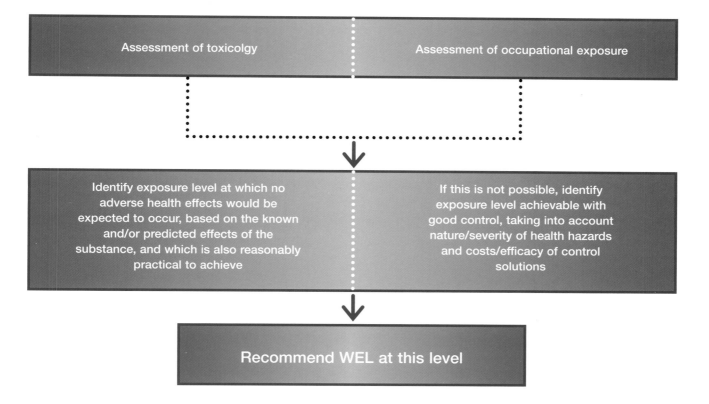

Applying occupational exposure limits

Scope of the limits

91   The list of WELs, unless otherwise stated, relates to personal exposure to substances hazardous to health in the air of the workplace. The limits cannot be adapted readily to evaluate or control non-occupational exposure, eg levels of contamination in the neighbourhood close to an industrial plant. WELs are approved only for application to people at work. Employers should also take into account their duties under the Environmental Protection Act (see http://www.environment-agency.gov.uk).[30] WELs are approved only for use where the atmospheric pressure is between 900 and 1100 millibars. This covers the normal range of meterological variations in Great Britain and slightly pressurised workplaces such as clean rooms, but not the hyperbaric conditions which may be encountered in, for example, tunneling or diving. To enable WELs to be applied in hyperbaric conditions the limits should be expressed as a partial pressure or mass/volume concentration at higher pressures. This approach has been endorsed by the Advisory Committee on Toxic Substances (ACTS) and is discussed in detail in EH75/2 *Occupational exposure limits for hyperbaric conditions.*[31]

92   Workplace exposure limits as set out in regulation 7 of COSHH, are intended to be used for normal working conditions in factories or other workplaces. Over and above their responsibilities to ensure that the requirements of COSHH are met, employers also have a clear responsibility to ensure that the plant is designed, operated and maintained in a way that avoids accidents and emergencies. Where appropriate, detection, alarm and response measures should be used in order to minimise the effect of any such unplanned events.

Long-term and short-term exposure limits

93   Effects of exposure to substances hazardous to health vary considerably depending on the nature of the substance and the pattern of exposure. Some effects require prolonged or accumulated exposure. The **long-term (8-hour TWA) exposure limit** is intended to control such effects by restricting the total intake by inhalation over one or more workshifts, depending on the length of the shift. Other effects may be seen after brief exposures. **Short-term exposure limits (usually 15 minutes)** may be applied to control these effects. For those substances for which no short-term limit is specified it is recommended that a figure of three times the long-term limit be used as a guideline for controlling short-term peaks in exposure. Some workplace activities give rise to frequent short (less than 15 minutes) periods of high exposure which, if averaged over time, do not exceed either an 8-hour TWA or a 15-minute TWA. Such exposures have the potential to cause harm and should be subject to reasonably practicable means of control unless a 'suitable and sufficient' risk assessment shows no risk to health from such exposures.

94   In some situations such as in submarines and saturation diving the occupational exposure is essentially continuous. In these cases a continuous exposure limit should be

derived by dividing the 8-hour TWA exposure limit by a factor of 5. This approach has been endorsed by ACTS and is discussed in detail in EH75/2 *Occupational exposure limits for hyperbaric conditions.*[31]

95   Both the long-term and short-term exposure limits are expressed as airborne concentrations averaged over a specified period of time. The period for the long-term limit is normally eight hours, when a different period is used this is stated. The averaging period for the short-term exposure limit is normally 15 minutes, such a limit applying to any 15-minute period throughout the working shift. Exposure to substances hazardous to health should be calculated according to the approved method, which is reproduced on pages 45-47.

Help in applying limits

COSHH essentials

96   HSE's guidance *COSHH essentials*[2] provides advice to employers on fulfilling a legal duty under COSHH to control exposures to chemicals hazardous to health. It uses a step-by-step process for identifying the right controls to reduce exposure for many hazardous substances, and control guidance sheets which apply to common situations, eg mixing, weighing, surface coating. In order to choose the correct control approach (general ventilation, engineering control, containment or special) the following factors are considered:

(a)   the possible health effects from exposure to a chemical. These are determined by the Risk Phrase for a substance (Table 1 includes a list of R-phrases). *COSHH essentials*[2] divides chemicals into five hazard bands. These range from A (least hazardous) through to E (most hazardous) with an additional band, S, which is used for substances that cause damage if they come into contact with the skin or eyes;

(b)   the amount of a chemical in use; and

(c)   its dustiness or volatility.

97   Once the general control approach is determined, more detailed advice can be found in dedicated control guidance sheets which cover a wide range of tasks.

98   The *COSHH essentials*[2] website (http://www.coshh-essentials.org.uk) now also provides direct advice for a number of tasks and processes in the production and service industries. This allows users to obtain advice without having to go through the assessment route. HSE plans to add further direct advice sheets to *COSHH essentials*.

99   For people who want more technical information to help them apply the scheme to hazards or situations, a summary of the technical basis for *COSHH essentials*[2] is available at http://www.coshh-essentials.org.uk/assets/live/CETB.pdf.

Units of measurement

100 In workplace exposure limits, concentrations of airborne particles (fume, dust etc) are usually expressed in $mg.m^{-3}$. In the case of dusts, the limits in the table refer to the 'inhalable' fraction unless specifically indicated as referring to the 'respirable' fraction (see paragraphs 42-45 on page 31). Exceptionally, the limits for MMMFs and for RCFs can be expressed either as $mg.m^{-3}$ or as fibres per millilitre of air ($fibres.ml^{-1}$) (see paragraphs 50-58 on pages 32-33 for asbestos). Workplace exposure limits for volatile substances are usually expressed in both parts per million by volume (ppm) and milligrams per cubic metre ($mg.m^{-3}$). For these substances, limits are set in ppm, and a conversion to $mg.m^{-3}$ is calculated. The value in $mg.m^{-3}$ for a given concentration in ppm depends on the temperature and pressure of the ambient air, which in reality vary over time. Therefore conversion calculations are based on a standard set of typical conditions.

Conversion and rounding of WELS expressed in ppm to mg.m^{-3}

101 The limits in Table 1 have been calculated from first principles, using the following method.

$$\text{WEL in } mg.m^{-3} = \frac{\text{WEL in ppm x MWt}}{24.05526}$$

where MWt is the molecular weight (molar mass in $g.mol^{-1}$) of the substance.

Note that 24.05526 $l.mol^{-1}$ is the molar volume of an ideal gas at 20°C and 1 atmosphere pressure (760 mm mercury, 101325 Pa, 1.01325 bar).

102 The results have been rounded using the following procedure:

Range containing the newly calculated WEL (in mg.m^{-3})	Round to:
Less than 0.1	1 significant figure
0.1 to less than 100	2 significant figures
100 or over	3 significant figures

Calculation of exposure

103 Exposure to substances hazardous to health should be calculated according to the approved method. The

calculated exposure should then be compared with the workplace exposure limits for that substance for the purposes of determining compliance with COSHH, regulation 7. Where a WEL is listed both for a long-term reference period and a short-term reference period it will be necessary to compare the calculated exposures appropriately with both workplace exposure limits.

skin absorption these factors should be taken into account in determining the adequacy of the control measures. Further guidance is given on the adequate control of exposure by routes other than inhalation in the COSHH ACOP,[5] in *The safe use of pesticides for non-agricultural purposes*[32] and *Code of practice for the safe use of pesticides on farms and holdings.*[33]

Limitations to the application of exposure limits

104 The exposure limits relate to personal monitoring.

Other factors

105 Working conditions which impose additional stress on the body, such as exposure to ultra-violet radiation, high temperatures, pressures and humidity, may increase the toxic response to a substance. In such cases specialist advice may be necessary to evaluate the effects of these factors.

Absorption through the skin

106 For most substances, the main route of entry into the body is by inhalation and the exposure limits given in this booklet relate solely to exposure by this route. However, some substances have the ability to penetrate intact skin and become absorbed into the body, thus contributing to systemic toxicity; these substances are marked in the table with an 'Sk' notation. ACTS has agreed the following criteria for assigning this notation:

(a)   The 'Sk' notation is assigned in cases where the available data or experience (or predictions made in the absence of actual data) suggest that exposure via the dermal route may:

(i)   make a substantial contribution to body burden (when compared to the contribution attributable to inhalation exposure at the WEL); and

(ii)   cause systemic effects, so that conclusions about exposure and health effects based solely on airborne concentration limits may be incomplete.

107 Absorption through the skin can result from localised contamination, for example from a splash on the skin or clothing, or in certain cases from exposure to high atmospheric concentrations of vapour. This may result in a substantial body burden, so that serious effects may result with little or no warning. It is necessary to take special precautions to prevent skin contact when handling these substances. Where the 'Sk' notation has been assigned and the methods of use provide a potential exposure route via

Calculation methods

Calculation of exposure with regard to the specified reference periods

108 This section reproduces the approved methods for the calculation of exposure in relation to the 8-hour, short-term and one-year reference periods. **These methods are legally binding because they have been approved by the Health and Safety Commission.**

Notice of approval

The Health and Safety Commission has on 9 November 2004 approved the methods of calculation set out in the Schedule to this Notice for the purpose of determining exposure in relation to the reference periods for workplace exposure limits as specified in regulation 2(1) of the Control of Substances Hazardous to Health Regulations 2002 (as amended) and occupational exposure limit for lead as specified in Regulation 2(1) of the Control of Lead at Work Regulations 2002.

Signed
SUSAN MAWER
Secretary to the Health and Safety Commission
9 November 2004

Schedule

Part 1 The 8-hour reference period

1   The term '8-hour reference period' relates to the procedure whereby the occupational exposures in any 24-hour period are treated as equivalent to a single uniform exposure for 8 hours (the 8-hour time-weighted average (TWA) exposure).

2   The 8-hour TWA may be represented mathematically by:

$$\frac{C_1 T_1 + C_2 T_2 + \ldots C_n T_n}{8}$$

where C_1 is the occupational exposure and T_1 is the associated exposure time in hours in any 24-hour period.

Example 1

3   The operator works for 7 hours 20 minutes on a process in which he is exposed to a substance hazardous to health. The average exposure during that period is measured as 0.12 mg.m^{-3}.

The 8-hour TWA =

> 7 h 20 min (7.33 h) at 0.12 mg.m^{-3}
> 40 min (0.67 h) at 0 mg.m^{-3}

That is

$$\frac{(0.12 \times 7.33) + (0 \times 0.67)}{8}$$

$$= 0.11 \text{ mg.m}^{-3}$$

Example 2

4   The operator works for eight hours on a process in which he is exposed to a substance hazardous to health. The average exposure during that period is measured as 0.15 mg.m^{-3}.

The 8-hour TWA =

$$\frac{(0.15 \times 8)}{8}$$

$$= 0.15 \text{ mg.m}^{-3}$$

Example 3

5   Working periods may be split into several sessions for the purpose of sampling to take account of rest and meal breaks etc. This is illustrated by the following example:

Working period	Exposure (mg.m^{-3})	Duration of sampling (h)
0800-1030	0.32	2.5
1045-1245	0.07	2
1330-1530	0.2	2
1545-1715	0.1	1.5

Exposure is assumed to be zero during the periods 1030 to 1045, 1245 to 1330 and 1530 to 1545.

The 8-hour TWA =

$$\frac{(0.32 \times 2.5) + (0.07 \times 2) + (0.20 \times 2) + (0.10 \times 1.5) + (0 \times 1.25)}{8}$$

$$\frac{0.80 + 0.14 + 0.40 + 0.15 + 0}{8}$$

$$= 0.19 \text{ mg.m}^{-3}$$

Example 4

6   An operator works for eight hours during the night shift on a process in which he is intermittently exposed to a substance hazardous to health. The operator's work pattern during the working period should be known and the best available data relating to each period of exposure should be applied in calculating the 8-hour TWA. These should be based on direct measurement, estimates based on data already available or reasonable assumptions.

Working period	Task	Exposure (mg.m^{-3})
2200 to 2400	Helping in workshop	0.1 (known to be exposure of full-time group in workshop)
2400 to 0100	Cleaning elsewhere in factory	0 (assumed)
0100 to 0400	Working in canteen	0 (assumed)
0400 to 0600	Cleaning-up after breakdown in workshop	0.21 measured

The 8-hour TWA =

$$\frac{(0.10 \times 2) + (0.21 \times 2) + (0 \times 4)}{8}$$

$$= 0.078 \text{ mg.m}^{-3}$$

Example 5

7   The operator works a 12-hour shift each day for five days, and then has seven days' rest. The exposure limits are based on an 8-hour reference period in each 24 hours in which an exposure occurs; the seven days' rest makes no difference. While at work, the operator is exposed to 4 mg.m^{-3}.

The 8-hour TWA=

$$\frac{(4 \times 12)}{8}$$

$$= 6 \text{ mg.m}^{-3}$$

The short-term reference period

8   Exposure should be recorded as the average over the specified short-term reference period, normally 15 minutes, and should be determined by sampling over that period. For short emissions of less than the reference period, which still may have the potential to cause harm, appropriate action should be taken to ensure that a 'suitable and sufficient' risk assessment is carried out to ensure that there is no risk to health from such exposures.

Methods of measurement and calculation for determining the fibre concentrations of MMMF

109 These paragraphs reproduce the Notice of Approval which is based on the methods detailed in MDHS59 *Man-made mineral fibre.*[34] **The methods are legally binding because they have been approved by the Health and Safety Commission.**

Notice of approval

The Health and Safety Commission has on 9 November 2004 approved the methods of measurement and calculation set out in the Schedule to this notice for the purpose of determining the fibre concentration of MMMF (also known as man-made mineral fibres, machine-made mineral fibres and man-made vitreous fibres) in air for comparison with the workplace exposure limit specified in the Health and Safety Commission's approved list of workplace exposure limits.

Signed:
SUSAN MAWER
Secretary to the Health and Safety Commission
9 November 2004

Schedule

1   The method shall measure the exposure of employees by sampling in the breathing zone of the employee exposed.

2   'Fibre' means a particle with a length >5 μm, average diameter <3 μm, and a ratio of length to diameter >3 to 1, which can be seen using the system specified in paragraph 3.

3   Fibres shall be counted with a phase contrast microscope of such a quality and maintained in such condition at all times during the use that Block 5 on the HSE/NPL Test Slide Mark II would be visible when used in accordance with the manufacturer's instructions. The microscope shall be tested with the Slide frequently enough to establish this. The microscope magnification shall be between 400x and 600x. During counting, the difference in

refractive index between the fibres and the medium in which they are immersed shall be between 0.05 and 0.30. The microscopist shall be properly trained in relevant techniques.

4   The results shall be regularly tested by quality assurance procedures to ensure that the results are in satisfactory agreement with the average of results obtained by British laboratories participating in a national quality assurance scheme using the methods specified in paragraphs 1-3.

Monitoring exposure

110 Regulation 10 of COSHH imposes a duty to monitor the exposure of employees to substances hazardous to health in certain specified situations. Further advice on these requirements may be found in the guidance on monitoring of exposure in the COSHH ACOP.[5]

Personal/workplace air monitoring

111 Sampling strategies may involve measurement of the hazardous substance in the breathing zone of the worker (personal sampling) or in the workplace air. Details of routine sampling strategies for individual substances are outside the scope of this document. However, advice is available in *Monitoring strategies for toxic substances*[6] which provides practical guidance on monitoring substances hazardous to health in air.

112 Methods for the sampling and analysis of many substances which have been assigned WELs are described in the HSE series 'Methods for the Determination of Hazardous Substances' (MDHS). The series also incorporates publications of a more general nature such as method validation protocols and guidance on analytical quality assessment and control.

113 HSE also operates an external quality assessment or proficiency testing scheme for the analysis of a range of common substances in workplace air. Details of the WASP scheme (Workplace Analysis Scheme for Proficiency), which is administered by HSE's Health and Safety Laboratory, are available through the HSE Information Centre (see paragraph 16).

Biological monitoring (see also Table 2, page 27)

114 Biological monitoring can be a very useful complementary technique to air monitoring when air sampling techniques alone may not give a reliable indication of exposure. Biological monitoring is the measurement and assessment of hazardous substances or their metabolites in tissues, secretions, excreta or expired air, or any combination of these, in exposed workers. Measurements reflect absorption of a substance by all routes. Biological monitoring may be particularly useful in circumstances where there is likely to be significant skin absorption and/or gastrointestinal tract uptake following ingestion; where control of exposure depends on respiratory protective equipment; where there is a reasonably well-defined relationship between biological monitoring and effect; or where it gives information on accumulated dose and target organ body burden which is related to toxicity.

115 Biological Monitoring Guidance Values (BMGVs) are set where they are likely to be of practical value, suitable monitoring methods exist and there are sufficient data available. The type of data that are available will vary between substances and therefore the route taken to deriving the BMGV will vary between substances. BMGVs are either based on a relationship between biological concentrations and health effects, between biological concentrations and exposure at the level of the WEL or are based on data collected from a representative sample of workplaces correctly applying the principles of good occupational hygiene practice. The technical basis for each BMGV will be clearly described in supporting documentation such as an EH64 summary or other guidance.

116 BMGVs are non-statutory and any biological monitoring undertaken in association with a guidance value needs to be conducted on a voluntary basis (ie with the fully informed consent of all concerned). BMGVs are intended to be used as tools in meeting the employer's primary duty to ensure adequate control under COSHH. Where a BMGV is exceeded it does not necessarily mean that any corresponding airborne standard has been exceeded nor that ill health will occur. It is intended that where they are exceeded this will give an indication that investigation into current control measures and work practices is necessary. Of course, that is not necessarily to say that because biological monitoring results are below a particular guidance value an employer need take no further action to reduce exposure. But it should be noted that BMGVs are not an alternative or replacement for airborne occupational exposure limits. Further guidance can be found in *Biological monitoring in the workplace*.[35]

Mixed exposures

WELs for mixtures

117 The majority of WELs listed in EH40 are for single compounds or for substances containing a common element or radical, for example, 'tungsten and compounds', and 'isocyanates'. A few of the WELs relate to substances commonly encountered as complex mixtures or compounds, for example 'rubber fume'. The WELs for complex mixtures such as rubber fume and hydrocarbon solvents (see paragraph 118) are without prejudice to any WELs for individual components. If the Safety Data Sheet lists a substance with a WEL, the employer should ensure that the WEL is not exceeded. If the substance is one to which a 'Carc' or 'Sen' notation has been applied or which is assigned one of the risk phrases R42, R42/43, R45, R46, R49, or is listed in Schedule 1 of the COSHH Regulations, or in section C of *Asthmagen? Critical assessments of the evidence for agents implicated in occupational asthma,* or is a substance which the risk assessment has shown to be a potential cause of occupational asthma there is a requirement to reduce exposure as low as is reasonably practicable. This requirement applies regardless of whether or not the substance has a WEL.

Hydrocarbon solvents

118 Hydrocarbon solvents are normally supplied as complex mixtures. To assist producers and suppliers of mixed hydrocarbon blends to determine suitable 'in house' OELs, ACTS recommend the procedure detailed in paragraphs 119-121. The supplier may pass this information on to a customer, and should in that case refer to this guidance. The procedure covers aliphatics in the range C_5 to C_{15}, cycloalkanes in the range C_5 to C_{16} and aromatics. This definition does **not** include halogenated or oxygenated hydrocarbons. The procedure only applies to vapours; mists are excluded.

Reciprocal calculation procedure for mixtures of hydrocarbon solvents

119 'In-house' OELs are derived using the reciprocal calculation procedure (RCP). Thus the OEL for a mixture is calculated as follows:

$$\frac{1}{OEL_{sol}} = \frac{FR_a}{OEL_a} + \frac{FR_b}{OEL_b} + \frac{FR_n}{OEL_n}$$

Where:

OEL_{sol} = occupational exposure limit of the hyrdocarbon solvent mixture (in $mg.m^{-3}$)

OEL_a = occupational exposure limit or guidance value of the component 'a' (in $mg.m^{-3}$)

FR_a = fraction (w/w) of component 'a' in the solvent mixture

The OEL_{sol} obtained should be rounded to the nearest number as follows:

OEL_{sol} <100 mg.m^{-3} nearest 25
              100-600 mg.m^{-3} nearest 50
              >600 mg.m^{-3} nearest 200

120 The RCP requires an OEL for each component in a mixture of hydrocarbons. Since for many individual hydrocarbons the data on which an OEL could be based is limited, ACTS agreed to:

(a) divide hydrocarbons into discrete groups based on structural similarity and critical health effects;

(b) exclude from these groups hydrocarbons with specific toxicity concerns (eg n-hexane). For these hydrocarbons WELs are listed in Table 1. These WELs should be used in the RCP;

(c) assign guidance values to these groups which can then be used in the RCP. It should be noted that guidance values have no legal status and there is no obligation on industry to comply with these values if they possess data indicating another limit is more appropriate.

The following values (8-hour TWAs) have been approved by ACTS:

Normal and branched chain alkanes

$C_5 - C_6$ 1800 mg.m^{-3}
$\geq C_7$ 1200 mg.m^{-3}

This group **excludes** n-hexane and n-heptane.

Cycloalkanes

$C_5 - C_6$ =   1800 mg.m^{-3}
$\geq C_7$ =   1200 mg.m^{-3}

This group **excludes** cyclohexane.

Aromatics

500 mg.m^{-3}

This group **excludes** benzene, toluene, xylene, (o-, m-, p- or mixed isomers), ethylbenzene, trimethylbenzene (all isomers) and cumene.

Example

121 The following is an example of how the RCP is applied. White spirit typically contains the following percentage of hydrocarbons:

52%   alkanes $\geq C_7$
      guidance value = 1200 mg.m^{-3}

27%   cycloalkanes $\geq C_7$
      guidance value = 800 mg.m^{-3}

10%   aromatics
      guidance value = 500 mg.m^{-3}

1% C_8 aromatics (o-, m-, p- xylene or mixed isomers) WEL = 220 mg.m^{-3}

10%   trimethybenzenes WEL = 125 mg.m^{-3}

Using the three guidance values and the WEL values for xylene and trimethybenzenes, an OEL for white spirit can be obtained as shown:

$$\frac{1}{OEL_{sol}} = \frac{52/100}{1200} + \frac{27/100}{800} + \frac{10/10}{500}$$

$$\frac{1/100}{220} + \frac{10/100}{125}$$

$$\frac{1}{OEL_{sol}} = 1.816 \times 10^{-3}$$

$$OEL_{sol} = 551 \text{ mg.m}^{-3}$$

rounded to the nearest 50 gives an OEL for this particular brand of white spirit of 550 mg.m^{-3}.

Effects of mixed exposures

122 In the workplace workers are frequently subject to a variety of mixed exposures involving solid or liquid aerosols or gases. These can arise as a result of work with materials containing a mixture of substances, or from work with several individual substances, simultaneously or successively, in a workshift. Mixed exposures require careful assessment of their health effects and the appropriateness of control standards. The following paragraphs provide a brief summary of the advice on the application of WELs in these circumstances. In all cases of doubt, specialist advice should be sought.

123 The ways in which the constituent substances of a mixed exposure interact vary considerably. Some mixed exposures involve substances that act on different body

tissues or organs, or by different toxicological mechanisms, these various effects being independent of each other. Other mixtures will include substances that act on the same organs, or by similar mechanisms, so that the effects reinforce each other and the substances are additive in their effect. In some cases the overall effect is considerably greater than the sum of the individual effects, and is synergistic. This may arise from mutual enhancements of the effects of the constituents or because one substance potentiates another, causing it to act in a way which it would not do alone.

Risk assessment and control

124 With all types of mixed exposures it is essential that assessments should be based on the concentrations of each of the constituents in air to which workers are exposed. Depending on the nature of the constituents and the circumstances of use, the relative concentrations of the constituents in air may differ considerably from those in the liquid or solid source material. The composition of the bulk material should not be relied on for assessment unless there is good evidence for doing so.

125 Where mixed exposures occur, the first step is to ensure adequate control of exposure for each individual substance, as explained in schedule 2A of the COSHH ACOP. WELs for defined mixtures should be used only where they are applicable and in addition to any relevant individual WELs. They should not be extended to inappropriate situations. It is then necessary to assess whether further control is needed to counteract any increased risk from the substances acting in conjunction. Expert assessments for some particular mixed exposures may be available and can be used as guidelines in similar cases. In other cases, close examination of the toxicological data will be necessary to determine which of the main types of interaction (if any) are likely for the particular combination of substances concerned; the various types should be considered in the following order:

(a) *Synergistic substances:* Known cases of synergism and potentiation are considerably less common than the other types of behaviour in mixed exposures. However, they are the most serious in their effects and require the most strict control. They are also the most difficult to assess and wherever there is reason to suspect such intervention, specialist advice should be obtained;

(b) *Additive substances:* Where there is reason to believe that the effects of the constituents are additive, and where the WELs are based on the same health effects the mixed exposure should be assessed by means of the formula:

$$C_1/L_1 + C_2/L_2 + C_3/L_3...<1$$

where C_1, C_2 etc are the time-weighted average (TWA) concentrations of constituents in air and L_1, L_2 are the corresponding WELs. Where the sum of the C/L fractions does not exceed 1, the exposure is considered not to exceed the notional exposure limit. The use of this formula is only applicable where L_1, L_2 etc relate to the same reference period in the list of approved WELs. This formula is not applicable where the lead health effect is cancer or asthma, ie substances to which a 'Carc' or 'Sen' notation has been applied or to which one of the risk phrases R42, R42/43, R45, R46, R49 has been assigned, or to substances listed in Schedule 1 of COSHH, or substances that are listed in section C of *Asthmagen? Critical assessments of the evidence for agents implicated in occupational asthma,*[4] or substances for which the risk assessment has shown to be a potential cause of occupational asthma. For mixtures containing these substances the overriding duty is to reduce exposure so far as is reasonably practicable (see paragraph 117).

(c) **Independent substances**: where no synergistic or additive effects are known or considered likely, the constituents can be regarded as acting independently and the measures needed to achieve adequate control assessed for each separately. The controls needed for the mixture will be those for the component requiring the tightest control.

126 The above steps provide a basic protocol for assessment of mixed exposures. It is open to people responsible for control of exposure to treat all non-synergistic systems as though they were additive. This avoids the need to distinguish additive and independent systems and can be regarded as the more prudent course, particularly where the toxicity data are scarce or difficult to assess.

Monitoring mixed exposure

127 Information on monitoring airborne contaminants is given in *Monitoring strategies for toxic substances.*[6] The number of components of a mixed exposure for which routine air monitoring is required can be reduced if their relative concentrations can be shown to be constant. This involves the selection of a key or marker, which may be one of the constituents, as a measure of the total contamination. Exposure to the marker is controlled at a level selected so that exposures to all components will be controlled in accordance with the criteria in paragraph 125 (a) and (b). However, if one of the components has been assigned a 'Carc' or 'Sen' notation or one of the risk phrases R42, R42/43, R45, R46, R49, or is listed in Schedule 1 of the COSHH regulations, or is listed in section C of *Asthmagen? Critical assessments of the evidence for agents implicated in occupational asthma,*[4] or is a

substance for which the risk assessment has shown to be a potential cause of occupational asthma, then the level of the exposure to that substance should always be reduced so far as is reasonably practicable. Monitoring should be under the guidance of suitable specialist advice.

Complicating factors

128 Several factors that complicate the assessment and control of exposure to individual substances will also affect cases of mixed exposures and will require similar special consideration. Such factors include:

(a)   exposure to a substance for which there is no WEL (see Schedule 2A of the COSHH ACOP);[5]

(b)   the relevance of such factors as alcohol, medication, smoking and additional stresses;

(c)   exposure of the skin to one or more substances that can be absorbed by this route as well as by inhalation (see Schedule 2A of the COSHH ACOP); and

(d)   substances in mixtures may mutually affect the extent of their absorption, as well as their health affects, at a given level of exposure.

In each of these circumstances specialist advice should be obtained.

List of synonyms

Substance	Name it is listed by in Table 1
α-chloropropylene oxide	1-Chloro-2, 3-epoxypropane (Epichlorohydrin)
(Diethylamine)ethane	Triethylamine
(S)-3-(1-Methyl-2-pyrrolidinyl)pyridine	Nicotine
1-(1-methylethyl)amino-3-(1-naphthalenoxy)propan-2-ol	Propranolol
1,1,1-trifluoro-2,2-chlorobromoethane	Halothane
1,1'-Azobiscarbamide	Azodicarbonamide
1,1'-Azobisformamide	Azodicarbonamide
1,1-Dichloroethylene	Vinylidene chloride
1,1'-Dimethyl-4,4'-Bipyridinium dichloride	Paraquat dichloride (ISO)
1,1-oxybisethane	Diethyl ether
1,2,3,4,7,7-Hexachloro-1,5,5a,6,9,9a-hexahydro-6, 9-methano-2,4,3-benzodioxathiepin-3-oxide	Endosulfan (ISO)
1,2,3-Trimethylbenzene	1,2,3-Trimethylbenzene
Hemi mellitene	Hemi mellitene
1,2,4-Benzenetricarboxylic anhydride	Trimellitic anhydride
1,2,4-TCB	1,2,4-Trichlorobenzene
1,2,4-Trimethylbenzene	1,2,4-Trimethylbenzene
Pseudocumene	Pseudocumene
1,2-Benzenedicarboxylic acid dinonyl ester	Dinonyl phthalate
1,2-Benzenedicarboxylic acid, di-2-propenyl ester	Diallyl phthalate
1,2-Benzenedicarboxylic anhydride	Phthalic anhydride
1,2-Benzenediol	Pyrocatechol
1,2-Bis(ethoxycarbonyl)ethyl O,O-dimethyl phosphorodithioate	Malathion (ISO)
1,2-Dichloroethene	1,2-Dichloroethylene, cistrans isomers 60:40
1,2-Dichlorotetrafluoroethane	Cryofluorane (INN)
1,2-Dihydroxybenzene	Pyrocatechol
1,2-Dihydroxyethane	Ethane-1,2-diol
1,2-Dihydroxypropane	Propane-1,2-diol
1,2-Epoxypropane	Propylene oxide
1,2-Ethanediol	Ethane-1,2-diol
1,3,5-Triglycidyl isocyanurate	Triglycidyl isocyanurate (TGIC)
1,3,5-Trimethylbenzene	1,3,5-Trimethylbenzene
Mesitylene	Mesitylene
1,3-Benzenediol	Resorcinol
1,3-Butadiene	Buta-1,3-diene
1,3-Dichloro-5,5-dimethyl-2,4-imidazolidinedione	1,3-Dichloro-5,5-dimethyl-hydantoin
1,3-Diformyl propane	Glutaraldehyde
1,3-Dioxo-5-phthalancarboxylic acid	Trimellitic anhydride
1,3-Dioxophthalan	Phthalic anhydride
1,3-Isobenzofurandione	Phthalic anhydride
1,3-Phthalandione	Phthalic anhydride
1,4,7-Tri-(aza)-heptane	2,2'-Iminodi (ethylamine)

Substance	Name it is listed by in Tabl
1,4-Benzenediamine	*p*-Phenylenediamine
1,4-Diaminobenzene	*p*-Phenylenediamine
1,4-Diazacyclohexane	Piperazine
1,4-Dihydroxybenzene	Hydroquinone
1,4-Epoxybutane	Tetrahydrofuran
1,7,7-Trimethylnorcamphor	Bornan-2-one
1-Amino-2-methylbenzene	o-Toluidine
1-Aminoethane	Ethylamine
1-Chloro-2,2,2-trifluoroethyldifluoromethyl ether	Isoflurane
1-Isopropylamino-3-(1-naphthyloxy)propan-2-ol	Propranolol
1-Methoxy-2-propanol acetate	1-Methoxypropyl acetate
1-Methoxypropylacetate-2-acetic acid	1-Methoxypropyl acetate
1-Methyl-2-aminobenzene	o-Toluidine
1-methyl-2-pyrrolidinone	1-Methyl-2-pyrrolidone
1-Methylethylbenzene	Cumene
1-pentyl acetate	Pentyl acetates (all isomers)
1-Propyl acetate	*n*-Propyl acetate
2,2-Bis(hydroxymethyl)-1,3-Propanediol	Pentaerythritol
2,4,6-Trinitrophenol	Picric acid
2,4-DES	Sodium 2-(2,4-dichlorophenoxy) ethyl sulphate
2,4-Dichlorophenoxyacetic acid	2,4-D (ISO)
2,5-Furandione	Maleic anhydride
2-Acetoxybenzoic acid	o-Acetylsalicylic acid
2-Acetoxypropane	Isopropyl acetate
2-Aminopyridine	2-Pyridylamine
2-Aminotoluene	o-Toluidine
2-Bromo-2-chloro-1,1,1-trifluroethane	Halothane
2-Butanone	Butan-2-one (methyl ethyl ketone)
2-Chloro-1,1,2-trifluoroethyldifluoromethyl ether	Enflurane
2-Chloro-1-ethanal	Chloroacetaldehyde
2-Ethylhexyl chlorocarbonate	2-Ethylhexyl chloroformate
2-Furacarboxyaldehde	2-furaldehyde (furfural)
2-Furanaldehyde	2-furaldehyde (furfural)
2-Furancarbonal	2-furaldehyde (furfural)
2-Hexanone	Hexan-2-one
2-Hydroxypropyl acrylate	2-Hydroxypropyl acrylate
2-Isopropoxyphenyl methylcarbamate	Propoxur (ISO)
2-Methoxy-1-methylethylacetate	1-Methoxypropyl acetate
2-Methoxy-2-methylpropane	Methyl-*tert*-butyl ether
2-Methyl-1-propyl acetate	Isobutyl acetate
2-Methyl-2-propenenitrile	Methacrylonitrile
2-Methyl-2-propenoic acid	Methyl methacrylate
2-Methylaniline	o-Toluidine
2-NP	2-Nitropropane
2-Oxohexamethylenimine	1,6-Hexanolactam (e-caprolactam)
2-Pentyl acetate	Pentyl acetates (all isomers)
2-Phenylpropane	Cumene
2-Propanol	Propan-2-ol
2-Propen-1-ol	Allyl alcohol

Substance	Name it is listed by in Table 1
2-Propenamide	Acrylamide
2-Propenenitrile	Acrylonitrile
2-Propenoic acid 2-cyano ethyl ester	Ethyl cyanoacrylate
2-Propenoic acid 2-cyano methyl ester	Methyl cyanoacrylate
2-Propenoic acid, n-butyl ester	n-Butyl acrylate
2-Propenoic ethyl ester	Ethyl acrylate
2-Toluidine	o-Toluidine
3-(3,4-Dichlorophenyl)-1,1-dimethylurea	Diuron (ISO)
3,3'-Dichloro-4,4'-diaminodiphenyl methane	2,2'-Dichloro-4, 4'-methylene dianiline (MbOCA)
3a,4,7,7a-Tetrahydro-4,7-methanoindene	Dicyclopentadiene
3-Heptanone	Heptan-3-one
3-Hydroxypropene	Allyl alcohol
3-pentyl acetate	Pentyl acetates (all isomers)
4,4'-Diaminodiphenylmethane	4,4'-Methylenedianiline
4,4'-Diamino-3,3'-dichlorodiphenylmethane	2,2'-Dichloro-4, 4'-methylene dianiline (MbOCA)
4,4-Methylene bis(2-chloroaniline)	2,2'-Dichloro-4, 4'-methylene dianiline (MbOCA)
4,4'-Thiobis(6-tert-butyl-m-cresol)	6,6'-Di-tert-butyl-4,4'-thiodi-m-cresol
4-Acetamidophenol	Paracetamol
4-Amino-3,5,6-trichloropyridine-2-carboxylic acid	Picloram (ISO)
4-Hydroxyacetanilide	Paracetamol
5-Bromo-3-sec-butyl-6-methyluracil	Bromacil (ISO)
Acetaminophen	Paracetamol
Acetanhydride	Acetic anhydride
Acetic acid amyl ester	Pentyl acetates (all isomers)
Acetic acid anhydride	Acetic anhydride
Acetic acid dimethylamide	NN-Dimethylacetamide
Acetic acid, 1,1-dimethylethyl ester	tert-Butyl acetate
Acetic aldehyde	Acetaldehyde
Acetic oxide	Acetic anhydride
Acetyl ether	Acetic anhydride
Acetyl oxide	Acetic anhydride
Acetylene dichloride	1,2-Dichloroethylene, cistrans isomers 60:40
Acetylene tetrabromide	1,1,2,2-Tetrabromoethane
Acrolein	Acrylaldehyde (Acrolein)
Acrylic acid 2-cyano ethyl ester	Ethyl cyanoacrylate
Acrylic acid 2-cyano methyl ester	Methyl cyanoacrylate
Acrylic acid, n-butyl ester	n-Butyl acrylate
ACT	Benzyl chloride
alpha-Chlorotoluene	Benzyl chloride
alpha-Methyl styrene	2-Phenylpropene
Alumina	Aluminium oxides
Aluminium alkyl compounds	Aluminium alkyl compounds
Aluminium metal	Aluminium metal
Aluminium salts, soluble	Aluminium salts, soluble
Alumite	Aluminium oxides
Aminobenzene	Aniline
Aminocaprolactam	1,6-Hexanolactam (e-caprolactam)
Aminocyclohexane	Cyclohexylamine
Aminoethane	Ethylamine
Ammonia, anhydrous	Ammonia, anhydrous

57

Substance	Name it is listed by in Table 1
Ammonium chloride, fume	Ammonium chloride, fume
Ammonium hexachloroplantinate	Halogeno-platinum compounds (as Pt)
Ammonium sulphamate	Ammonium sulphamidate
Ammonium tetrachloroplantinate	Halogeno-platinum compounds (as Pt)
Amyl acetates (all isomers)	Pentyl acetates (all isomers)
Amyl ethyl ketone	5-Methylheptan-3-one
Amylmethylketone	Heptan-2-one
Antimony and compounds except stibine (as Sb)	Antimony and compounds except stibine (as Sb)
Araldite PT-810	Triglycidyl isocyanurate (TGIC)
Arcton 22	Chlorodifluoromethane
Aroclor	Polychlorinated biphenyls (PCB)
Arsenic and arsenic compounds except arsine (as As)	Arsenic and arsenic compounds except arsine (as As)
Arsenic trihydride	Arsine
Arylamine	Aniline
Asphalt, petroleum fumes	Asphalt, petroleum fumes
Aspirin	o-Acetylsalicylic acid
Azabenzene	Pyridine
Azacyclohexane	Piperidine
Barite	Barium sulphate
Barium Compounds	Barium Compounds
Barytes	Barium sulphate
BCME	Bis(chloromethyl ether)
Benzenamine	Aniline
Benzene chloride	Chlorobenzene
Benzol	Benzene
Benzoyl peroxide	Dibenzoyl peroxide
Beryllium and beryllium compounds (as Be)	Beryllium and beryllium compounds (as Be)
Beta-propanolol	Propranolol
Bicyclo(2,2,1)heptan-2-one	Bornan-2-one
Bismuth telluride	Dibismuth tritelluride
Bladafum	Sulfotep (ISO)
Blanc fixe	Barium sulphate
Borates, (tetra) sodium salts	Disodium tetraborate, anhydrous
Borates, (tetra) sodium salts	Disodium tetraborate, decahydrate
Borates, (tetra) sodium salts	Disodium tetraborate, pentahydrate
Boron oxide	Diboron trioxide
Boron tribromide	Boron tribromide
Bromine	Bromine
Butane	Butane
Butanone	Butan-2-one (methyl ethyl ketone)
Butyl acrylate	n-Butyl acrylate
Butyl benzyl phthalate	Benzyl butyl phthalate
Butyl cellosolve	2-Butoxyethanol
Butyl cellosolve acetate	2-Butoxyethyl acetate
Butyl ethyl ketone	Heptan-3-one
Butyl glycol	2-Butoxyethanol
Butyl glycol acetate	2-Butoxyethyl acetate
Butyl methyl ketone	Hexan-2-one
Butyl oxitol	2-Butoxyethanol
Butyl phosphate	Tributyl phosphate, all isomers

Substance	Name it is listed by in Table 1
Butylated hydroxytoluene	2,6-Di-tert-butyl-p-cresol
Butylene oxide	Tetrahydrofuran
Butylglycol acetate	2-Butoxyethyl acetate
C,C'-azodi(formamide)	Azodicarbonamide
Cadmium & cadmium compounds except cadmium oxide fume, cadmium sulphide & cadmium sulphide pigments	Cadmium & cadmium compounds except cadmium oxide fume, cadmium sulphide & cadmium sulphide pigments
Cadmium oxide fume (as Cd)	Cadmium oxide fume (as Cd)
Cadmium sulphide and cadmium sulphide pigments (respirable dust (as Cd))	Cadmium sulphide and cadmium sulphide pigments (respirable dust (as Cd))
Caesium hydroxide	Caesium hydroxide
Calcite	Marble
Calcium carbonate	Calcium carbonate
Calcium cyanamide	Calcium cyanamide
Calcium hydroxide	Calcium hydroxide
Calcium oxide	Calcium oxide
Calcium silicate	Calcium silicate
Calcium sulphate	Gypsum
Calcium sulphate	Plaster of Paris
Camphor, synthetic	Bornan-2-one
Caprolactam	1,6-Hexanolactam (e-caprolactam)
Carbamaldehyde	Formamide
Carbimides	Isocyanates
Carbodiimide	Cyanamide
Carbon bisulphide	Carbon disulphide
Carbon black	Carbon black
Carbon oxychloride	Phosgene
Carbonic anhydride	Carbon Dioxide
Carbonic oxide	Carbon monoxide
Carbonimides	Isocyanates
Carbonyl chloride	Phosgene
Carbylamines	Isocyanates
Catechol	Pyrocatechol
Cellosolve	2-Ethoxyethanol
Cellosolve acetate	2-Ethoxyethyl acetate
Cellulose	Cellulose (pure)
Cement dust	Portland cement
CFC-114	Cryofluorane (INN)
Chlorinated biphenyls	Polychlorinated biphenyls (PCB)
Chlorine	Chlorine
Chlorine (IV) oxide	Chlorine dioxide
Chlorine oxide	Chlorine dioxide
Chlorine peroxide	Chlorine dioxide
Chloroacetic acid	Monochloroacetic acid
Chlorobenzol	Chlorobenzene
Chlorocyanogen	Cyanogen chloride
Chloroethylene	Vinyl chloride
Chloromethyl ether	Bis (chloromethyl ether)
Chloromethyloxirane	1-Chloro-2, 3-epoxypropane (Epichlorohydrin)
Chlorophenylmethane	Benzyl chloride
Chlorosulphonic acid	Chlorosulphonic acid

Substance	Name it is listed by in Table 1
Chromium	Chromium
Chromium (II) compounds	Chromium (II) compounds
Chromium (III) compounds	Chromium (III) compounds
Chromium (VI) compounds (as Cr)	Chromium (VI) compounds (as Cr)
Cinerin	Pyrethrins (ISO)
cis-Butenedioic anhydride	Maleic anhydride
Cobalt and cobalt compounds (as Co)	Cobalt and cobalt compounds (as Co)
Colophony	Rosin-based solder flux fume
Copper	Copper
Cotton dust	Cotton dust
Cristobalite, respirable dust	Silica, respirable crystalline
Crystalline silica, respirable dust	Silica, respirable crystalline
Cyanides, except HCN, cyanogen & cyanogen chloride	Cyanides, except HCN, cyanogen & cyanogen chloride
Cyanoethylene	Acrylonitrile
Cyanolit	Methyl cyanoacrylate
Cyanomethane	Acetonitrile
Cyclohexane	Cyclohexane
Cyclohexanone isooxime	1,6-Hexanolactam (e-caprolactam)
Dactin	1,3-Dichloro-5,5-dimethyl-hydantoin
DADPM	4,4'-Methylenedianiline
DDM	4,4'-Methylenedianiline
DEHP	Bis(2-ethylhexyl) phthalate
Derris, commercial	Rotenone (ISO)
Diacetone alcohol	4-Hydroxy-4-methylpentan-2-one
Dialkyl 79 phthalate	Dialkyl 79 phthalate
Diamine	Hydrazine
Diatomaceous earth, natural, respirable dust	Diatomaceous earth, natural, respirable dust
Diazenedicarboxamide	Azodicarbonamide
Dibutyl phthalate	Dibutyl phthalate
Dichloroacetylene	Dichloroacetylene
Dicyclohexyl phthalate	Dicyclohexyl phthalate
Diethyl ketone	Pentan-3-one
Diethyl oxide	Diethyl ether
Diethyl phthalate	Diethyl phthalate
Diethylene glycol	2,2'-Oxydiethanol
Diethylene imidoximine	Morpholine
Diethylene oxide	Tetrahydrofuran
Diethylene oximine	Morpholine
Diethylene triamine	2,2'-Iminodi (ethylamine)
Diethylenediamine	Piperazine
Diethylenediamine dihydrochloride	Piperazine dihydrochloride
Diethyleneimine	Piperazine
Difluorochloromethane	Chlorodifluoromethane
Diisobutyl ketone	2,6-Dimethylheptan-4-one
Diisobutyl phthalate	Diisobutyl phthalate
Diisodecyl phthalate	Diisodecyl phthalate
Diisononyl phthalate	Diisononyl phthalate
Diisooctyl phthalate	Diisooctyl phthalate
Diisopropylamine	Diisopropylamine
Dimethyl ketone	Acetone

Substance	Name it is listed by in Table 1
Dimethyl phthalate	Dimethyl phthalate
Dimethyl sulphate	Dimethyl sulphate
Dimethylbenzene	Xylene, o-,m-,-p- or mixed isomers
Dimethylethanolamine	Dimethylaminoethanol
Dimethylethylamine	N,N-Dimethylethylamine
Dimethylnitromethane	2-Nitropropane
Di-n-butyl phosphate	Dibutyl hydrogen phosphate
Dinitrobenzene, all isomers	Dinitrobenzene, all isomers
Dinitrogen monoxide	Nitrous oxide
Dioxan	1,4-Dioxane
Diphenylamine	Diphenylamine
Dipropylene glycol methyl ether	(2-methoxymethylethoxy) propanol
Dipropylene glycol monomethyl ether	(2-methoxymethylethoxy) propanol
Dipropylmethane	n-Heptane
Dipyrido[1,2-a:2',1'-c]pyrazinediium, 6,7-dihydro-, dibromide	Diquat dibromide (ISO)
Di-sec-octyl phthalate	Bis(2-ethylhexyl) phthalate
Dithiocarbonic anhydride	Carbon disulphide
Dithiofos	Sulfotep (ISO)
Dithiophosphoric acid, tetraethyl ester	Sulfotep (ISO)
Dithiotep	Sulfotep (ISO)
Divanadium pentoxide	Vanadium pentoxide
DMA	NN-Dimethylacetamide
DMAc	NN-Dimethylacetamide
DMAE	Dimethylaminoethanol
DME	Dimethyl ether
DMEA	Dimethylaminoethanol
DMF	Dimethylformamide
DMS	Dimethyl sulphate
DPGME	(2-methoxymethylethoxy) propanol
Dursban	Chlorpyrifos (ISO)
EAK	5-Methylheptan-3-one
EBK	Heptan-3-one
ECA	Ethyl cyanoacrylate
e-Caprolactam	1,6-Hexanolactam (e-caprolactam)
ECH	1-Chloro-2, 3-epoxypropane (Epichlorohydrin)
EDB	1,2-Dibromoethane (Ethylene dibromide)
Emery	Emery
Enthrane	Enflurane
Epichlorohydrin	1-Chloro-2, 3-epoxypropane (Epichlorohydrin)
Epoxyethane	Ethylene oxide
Ethanal	Acetaldehyde
Ethanamine	Ethylamine
Ethanedioic acid	Oxalic acid
Ethanediol	Ethane-1,2-diol
Ethanoic anhydride	Acetic anhydride
Ethanolamine	2-Aminoethanol
Ether	Diethyl ether
Ether hydrochloric	Chlorethane
Ethrane	Enflurane
Ethyl 2-propenoate	Ethyl acrylate

Substance	Name it is listed by in Table 1
Ethyl acetate	Ethyl acetate
Ethyl acetate ester	Ethyl acetate
Ethyl alcohol	Ethanol
Ethyl aldehyde	Acetaldehyde
Ethyl amyl ketone	5-Methylheptan-3-one
Ethyl butyl ketone	Heptan-3-one
Ethyl chloride	Chloroethane
Ethyl chlorocarbonate	Ethyl chloroformate
Ethyl ethanoate	Ethyl acetate
Ethyl ether	Diethyl ether
Ethyl mercaptan	Ethanethiol
Ethyl methanoate	Ethyl formate
Ethyl oxide	Diethyl ether
Ethyl thiopyrophosphate	Sulfotep (ISO)
Ethyl-2-cyano-2-propenoate	Ethyl cyanoacrylate
Ethyl-2-cyanoacrylate	Ethyl cyanoacrylate
Ethylene chlorohydrin	2-Chloroethanol
Ethylene dibromide	1,2-Dibromoethane (Ethylene dibromide)
Ethylene dichloride	1,2-Dichloroethane (Ethylene dichloride)
Ethylene glycol	Ethane-1,2-diol
Ethylene glycol dimethyl ether	Dimethoxymethane
Ethylene glycol monobutyl ether	2-Butoxyethanol
Ethylene glycol monobutyl ether acetate	2-Butoxyethyl acetate
Ethylene glycol monoethyl ether	2-Ethoxyethanol
Ethylene glycol monoethyl ether acetate	2-Ethoxyethyl acetate
Ethylene glycol monomethyl ether	2-Methoxyethanol
Ethylene glycol monomethyl ether acetate	2-Methoxyethyl acetate
Ethylene tetrachloride	Tetrachloroethylene
Ethylidene chloride	1,1-Dichloroethane
Ethylidene dichloride	1,1-Dichloroethane
Ferric oxide	Rouge
Ferrous foundry particulate	Ferrous foundry particulate
Flour dust	Flour Dust
Flue gas	Carbon monoxide
Fluoride (inorganic as F)	Fluoride (inorganic as F)
Fluorine	Fluorine
Fluothane	Halothane
Forane	Isoflurane
Formic aldehyde	Formaldehyde
Freon 123B1	Halothane
Freon 134a	1,1,1,2-Tetrafluoroethane (HFC 134a)
Freon 22	Chlorodifluoromethane
Fural	2-furaldehyde (furfural)
Furfural	2-furaldehyde (furfural)
Furfuraldehyde	2-furaldehyde (furfural)
Germanium tetrahydride	Germane
Glutaral	Glutaraldehyde
Glutardialdehyde	Glutaraldehyde
Glutaric dialdehyde	Glutaraldehyde
Glycerin, mist	Glycerol, mist

Substance	Name it is listed by in Table 1
Glycol	Ethane-1,2-diol
Grain dust	Grain dust
Graphite	Graphite
Halane	1,3-Dichloro-5,5-dimethyl-hydantoin
Halogeno-platinum compounds (complex co-ordination compounds in which the platinum atom is directly co-ordinated to halide groups) (as Pt)	Halogeno-platinum compounds (complex co-ordination compounds in which the platinum atom is directly co-ordinated to halide groups) (as Pt)
Hardwood dust	Hardwood dust
HCFC 22	Chlorodifluoromethane
HCFC-21	Dichlorofluoromethane
Heavy spar	Barium sulphate
Hexahydro-1,4-diazine	Piperazine
Hexahydro-2H-azepin-2-one	1,6-Hexanolactam (e-caprolactam)
Hexahydrobenzene	Cyclohexane
Hexahydropyrazine	Piperazine
Hexalin	Cyclohexanol
Hexamethylene	Cyclohexane
Hexane	n-Hexane
Hexanon	Cyclohexanone
Hexylene glycol	2-Methylpentane-2,4-diol
HFC 134a	1,1,1,2-Tetrafluoroethane
Hydrobromic acid	Hydrogen bromide
Hydrobromic gas	Hydrogen bromide
Hydrochloric acid	Hydrogen chloride (gas and aerosol mists)
Hydrocyanic acid	Hydrogen cyanide
Hydrofluoric acid	Hydrogen fluoride (as F)
Hydrofuran	Tetrahydrofuran
Hydrogen peroxide	Hydrogen peroxide
Hydrogen phosphide	Phosphine
Hydrogen selenide	Dihydrogen selenide (as Se)
Hydrosulphuric acid	Hydrogen sulphide
Hydrous magnesium silicate	Talc
Hydroxybenzene	Phenol
Indium and compounds (as In)	Indium and compounds (as In)
Indonaphthene	Indene
Iodine	Iodine
Iron oxide, fume (as Fe)	Iron oxide, fume (as Fe)
Iron pentacarbonyl (as Fe)	Pentacarbonyliron (as Fe)
Iron salts (as Fe)	Iron salts (as Fe)
Isoamyl alcohol	3-Methylbutan-1-ol
Isoamyl methyl ketone	5-Methylhexan-2-one
Isobutyl alcohol	2-Methylpropan-1-ol
Isocyanates, all (as –NCO)	Isocyanates, all (as –NCO)
Isocyanic acid esters	Isocyanates
Isonitropropane	2-Nitropropane
Isooctanol	Isooctyl alcohol (mixed isomers)
Isopentyl acetate	Pentyl acetates (all isomers)
Isopentyl methyl ketone	5-Methylhexan-2-one
Isophorone	3,5,5-trimethylcyclohex-2-enone
Isopropanol	Propan-2-ol

Substance	Name it is listed by in Table 1
Isopropyl acetone	4-Methylpentan-2-one
Isopropyl alcohol	Propan-2-ol
Isopropyl chlorocarbonate	Isopropyl chloroformate
Isopropyl ether	Diisopropyl ether
Isopropylbenzene	Cumene
Jasmolin	Pyrethrins (ISO)
Kaolin, respirable dust	Kaolin, respirable dust
Ketohexamethylene	Cyclohexanone
Laughing gas	Nitrous oxide
Limestone	Limestone
Lithium hydride	Lithium hydride
Lithium hydroxide	Lithium hydroxide
LPG	Liquefied petroleum gas
Magnesia	Magnesium oxide (as Mg)
Magnesium carbonate	Magnesite
Maleic acid anhydride	Maleic anhydride
Manganese and its inorganic compounds	Manganese and its inorganic compounds
MbOCA	2,2'-Dichloro-4,4'-methylene dianiline (MbOCA)
MCA	Methyl cyanoacrylate
MDA	4,4'-Methylenedianiline
m-Dihydroxybenzene	Resorcinol
Mecrylate	Methyl cyanoacrylate
MEK	Butan-2-one (methyl ethyl ketone)
MEKP	Methyl ethyl ketone peroxides (MEKP)
Methacide	Toluene
Methacrylic acid methyl ester	Methyl methacrylate
Methanal	Formaldehyde
Methanamide	Formamide
Methane trichloride	Chloroform
Methanoic acid	Formic Acid
Methyl 2-methyl-2-propenoate	Methyl methacrylate
Methyl acetate	Methyl acetate
Methyl alcohol	Methanol
Methyl aldehyde	Formaldehyde
Methyl bromide	Bromomethane
Methyl butyl ketone	Hexan-2-one
Methyl cellosolve	2-Methoxyethanol
Methyl cellosolve acetate	2-Methoxyethyl acetate
Methyl chloride	Chloromethane
Methyl chloroform	1,1,1-Trichloroethane
Methyl ester	Methyl methacrylate
Methyl ether	Dimethyl ether
Methyl ethyl ketone	Butan-2-one (methyl ethyl ketone)
Methyl ethylene oxide	Propylene oxide
Methyl iodide	Iodomethane
Methyl isoamyl ketone	5-Methylhexan-2-one
Methyl isobutyl carbinol	4-Methylpentan-2-ol
Methyl isobutyl ketone	4-Methylpentan-2-one
Methyl ketone	Acetone
Methyl mercaptan	Methanethiol

Substance	Name it is listed by in Table 1
Methyl n-butyl ketone	Hexan-2-one
Methyl phosphite	Trimethyl phosphite
Methyl propyl ketone	Pentan-2-one
Methyl-1,1-dimethyethyl ether	Methyl-tert-butyl ether
Methyl-2-cyano-2-propenoate	Methyl cyanoacrylate
Methyl-2-cyanoacrylate	Methyl cyanoacrylate
Methylacetic acid	Propionic acid
Methylacetone	Butan-2-one (methyl ethyl ketone)
Methylal	Dimethoxymethane
Methylamylketone	Heptan-2-one
Methylaniline	N-Methylaniline
Methylbenzene	Toluene
Methylbutyl acetate	Pentyl acetates (all isomers)
Methyldichloromethane	1,1-Dichloroethane
Methylene chloride	Dichloromethane
Methylene oxide	Formaldehyde
Methylene-bis-orthochloroaniline MbOCA	2,2'-Dichloro-4, 4'-methylene dianiline (MbOCA)
Methylhexalin	Methylcyclohexanol
Methyloxirane	Propylene oxide
MIAK	5-Methylhexan-2-one
MIBK	4-Methylpentan-2-one
MMMFs	MMMF (Machine-made mineral fibre) (except for Refractory Ceramic Fibres and Special Purpose Fibres)
Molybdenum compounds (as Mo)	Molybdenum compounds (as Mo)
Monochlorobenzene	Chlorobenzene
Monochlorodifluoromethane	Chlorodifluoromethane
Monoethylamine	Ethylamine
M-Pyrol	1-Methyl-2-pyrrolidone
MTBE	Methyl-tert-butyl ether
Muriatic acid	Hydrogen chloride (gas and aerosol mists)
N-(4-Hydroxyphenyl)acetamide	Paracetamol
N,N-diethylethanamine	Triethylamine
N,N-Diethylethanolamine	2-Dimethylaminoethanol
N,N-Dimethylethanolamnie	Dimethylaminoethanol
N,N-Dimethylformamide	Dimethylformamide
Nadone	Cyclohexanone
n-Butanol	Butan-1-ol
n-Butyl acetate	Butyl acetate
n-Butyl alcohol	Butan-1-ol
n-Butyl chlorocarbonate	n-Butyl chloroformate
n-Butyl lactate	Butyl lactate
N-Diethylaminoethanol	2-Dimethylaminoethanol
N-Ethylethanamine	Diethylamine
N-Ethylmorpholine	4-Ethylmorpholine
Nickel and its inorganic compounds (except nickel carbonyl)	Nickel and its inorganic compounds (except nickel carbonyl)
Nickel and its inorganic compounds (except nickel tetracarbonyl): water-soluble nickel compounds (as Ni) nickel and water-insoluble nickel compounds (as Ni)	Nickel and its inorganic compounds (except nickel tetracarbonyl): water-soluble nickel compounds (as Ni) nickel and water-insoluble nickel compounds (as Ni)

Substance	Name it is listed by in Table 1
Nickel carbonyl	Tetracarbonylnickel
Nitric Acid	Nitric Acid
Nitrobenzol	Nitrobenzene
Nitroisopropane	2-Nitropropane
Nitromethane	Nitromethane
N-methyl-2-pyrrolidinone	1-Methyl-2-pyrrolidone
N-Methylmethanamine	Dimethylamine
N-methylpyrrolidone	1-Methyl-2-pyrrolidone
n-Propanol	Propan-1-ol
N-Trichloromethylmercapto-4-cyclohexene-1,2-dicarboximide	Captan (ISO)
O,O,O',O'-Tetraethyldithio-pyrophosphate	Sulfotep (ISO)
O,O-Diethyl O-3,5,6-trichloro-2-pyridyl phosphorothioate	Chlorpyrifos (ISO)
O,O-Diethyl S-ethylthiomethyl phosphorodithioate	Phorate (ISO)
o-Dichlorobenzene	1,2-Dichlorobenzene (ortho-dichlorobenzene)
omega-Chlorotoluene	Benzyl chloride
o-Methylcyclohexanone	2-Methylcyclohexanone
Orsin	p-Phenylenediamine
ortho-Dichlorobenzene	1,2-Dichlorobenzene
o-sec-Butylphenol	2-sec-Butylphenol
Osmium tetraoxide (as Os)	Osmium tetraoxide (as Os)
Oxirane	Ethylene oxide
Oxomethane	Formaldehyde
Oxybis(chloromethane)	Bis (chloromethyl ether)
Oxybismethane	Dimethyl ether
Oxymethylene	Formaldehyde
p-Aminoaniline	p-Phenylenediamine
para-Dichlorobenzene	1,4-Dichlorobenzene
Paraffin wax, fume	Paraffin wax, fume
PCBs	Polychlorinated biphenyls (PCB)
p-Chloronitrobenzene	1-Chloro-4-nitrobenzene
p-Dichlorobenzene	1,4-Dichlorobenzene (para-dichlorobenzene)
Pentan-1,5-dial	Glutaraldehyde
Perc	Tetrachloroethylene
Perchloroethylene	Tetrachloroethylene
Periclase	Magnesium oxide (as Mg)
PGME	1-Methoxypropan-2-ol
PGMEA	1-Methoxypropyl acetate
Phenacyl chloride	2-Chloroacetophenone
Phenyl chloride	Chlorobenzene
Phenyl ether	Diphenyl ether (vapour)
Phenylamine	Aniline
Phenylethane	Ethylbenzene
Phenylethylene	Styrene
Phenylmethane	Toluene
Phosphoric acid	Orthophosphoric acid
Phosphoric chloride	Phosphorus pentachloride
Phosphorous chloride	Phosphorus trichloride
Phosphorus (V) oxide	Diphosporus pentoxide
Phosphorus pentasulphide	Diphosphorus pentasulphide

Substance	Name it is listed by in Table 1
Phosphorus pentoxide	Diphosphorus pentoxide
Phosphorus perchloride	Phosphorus pentachloride
Phosphorus trihydride	Phosphine
Phosphorus, yellow	Phosphorus, yellow
Phosphoryl trichloride	Phosphoryl trichloride
Phosporus pentoxide	Diphosporus pentoxide
Phthalic acid anhydride	Phthalic anhydride
Pimelic ketone	Cyclohexanone
Piperazidine	Piperazine
Piperazine hydrochloride	Piperazine dihydrochloride
Platinum compds, soluble (except certain halogeno-Pt compounds) (as Pt)	Platinum compds, soluble (except certain halogeno-Pt compounds) (as Pt)
Platinum metal	Platinum metal
p-Nitrochlorobenzene	1-Chloro-4-nitrobenzene
Polychlorobiphenyls	Polychlorinated biphenyls (PCB)
Polymeric aromatic amide derivative	p-Aramid respirable fibres
Potassium hydroxide	Potassium hydroxide
p-Phenylene terephthalamide	p-Aramid respirable fibres
Precipitator ash	Pulverised fuel ash
Propan-2-one	Acetone
Propanoic acid	Propionic acid
Propanone	Acetone
Propene oxide	Propylene oxide
Propenol	Allyl alcohol
Propenol alcohol	Allyl alcohol
Propionic acid	Propionic acid
Propylene glycol	Propane-1,2-diol
Propylene glycol methyl ether	1-Methoxypropan-2-ol
Propylene glycol methyl ether acetate	1-Methoxypropyl acetate
Propylene glycol-1-monomethyl ether	1-Methoxypropan-2-ol
Propylene glycol-1-monomethylether-2-acetate	1-Methoxypropyl acetate
Prussic acid	Hydrogen cyanide
PVC	Polyvinyl chloride
Pyrazine hexahydride	Piperazine
Pyrethrin	Pyrethrins (ISO)
Pyrethrins (Pyrethrum)	Pyrethrins (Pyrethrum)
Pyridinecarboxylic acid	Picloram (ISO)
Pyromucic aldehyde	2-furaldehyde (furfural)
Quartz, crystyalline	Silica, respirable crystalline
Quinol	Hydroquinone
RCF	Refractory Ceramic Fibres and Special Purpose Fibres
Resorcin	Resorcinol
Respirable Crystalline Silica (RCS)	Respirable Crystalline Silica (RCS)
Rhodium (as Rh)	Rhodium (as Rh)
Rubber fume	Rubber fume
Rubber process dust	Rubber process dust
sec-Butanol	Butan-2-ol
sec-Butyl acetate	sec-Butyl acetate
sec-Butyl alcohol	Butan-2-ol
Selane	Dihydrogen selenide (as Se)
Selenium and compounds, except hydrogen selenide (as Se)	Selenium and compounds, except hydrogen selenide (as Se)

Substance	Name it is listed by in Table 1
Selenium dihydride	Dihydrogen selenide (as Se)
Selenium hydride	Dihydrogen selenide (as Se)
Sextone	Cyclohexanone
Silane	Silane
Silica, amorphous	Silica, amorphous
Silica, fused respirable dust	Silica, fused respirable dust
Silicon	Silicon
Silicon carbide (not whiskers)	Silicon carbide (not whiskers)
Silver (soluble compounds as Ag)	Silver (soluble compounds as Ag)
Silver compounds	Silver compounds
Silver, metallic	Silver, metallic
Soapstone	Mica
Sodium azide (as NaN_3)	Sodium azide (as NaN_3)
Sodium bisulphite	Sodium hydrogen sulphite
Sodium hydroxide	Sodium hydroxide
Sodium metabisuphite	Disodium disulphite
Sodium pyrophosphate	Tetrasodium pyrophosphate
Softwood dust	Softwood dust
Starch	Starch
Styrol	Styrene
Subtilisins	Subtilisins
Sulphur hexafluoride	Sulphur hexafluoride
Sulphur monochloride	Disulphur dichloride
Sulphur oxychloride	Thionyl chloride
Sulphuretted hydrogen	Hydrogen sulphide
Sulphuric acid diethyl ester	Diethyl sulphate
Sulphuric acid, dimethyl ester	Dimethyl sulphate
Sulphuryl fluoride	Sulphuryl difluoride
Suphuric oxyfluoride	Sulphuryl difluoride
sym-Dichlorodimethyl ether	Bis (chloromethyl ether)
sym-Dichloroethane	1,2-Dichloroethane (Ethylene dichloride)
sym-Dichoroethylene	1,2-Dichloroethylene, cistrans isomers 60:40
Talc, respirable dust	Talc, respirable dust
Talcum	Talc
Tantalum	Tantalum
TEDP	Sulfotep (ISO)
Tellurium & compounds, except hydrogen telluride, (as Te)	Tellurium & compounds, except hydrogen telluride, (as Te)
Terphenyls, all isomers	Terphenyls, all isomers
tert-amyl acetate)	Pentyl acetates (all isomers)
tert-Butyl alcohol	2-Methylpropan-2-ol
tert-Butyl methyl ether	Methyl-tert-butyl ether
Tetrachloroethene	Tetrachloroethylene
Tetrachloromethane	Carbon tetrachloride
Tetrahydro-1,4-oxazine	Morpholine
TGIC	Triglycidyl isocyanurate (TGIC)
Thallium, soluble compounds (as Tl)	Thallium, soluble compounds (as Tl)
Thioglycolic acid	Mercaptoacetic acid
Thiosulfan	Endosulfan (ISO)
Tin compounds, inorganic, except SnH_4, (as Sn)	Tin compounds, inorganic, except SnH4, (as Sn)
Tin compounds, organic, except Cyhexatin (ISO), (as Sn)	Tin compounds, organic, except Cyhexatin (ISO), (as Sn)
Titanium dioxide	Titanium dioxide

Substance	Name it is listed by in Table 1
TMA	Trimellitic anhydride
TNT	2,4,6-Trinitrotoluene
Toluol	Toluene
Tolyl chloride	Benzyl chloride
Tosyl chloride	p-Toluenesulphonyl chloride
Toxilic anhydride	Maleic anhydride
Triatomic oxygen	Ozone
Trichloroethene	Trichloroethylene
Trichloromethane	Chloroform
Triiodomethane	Iodoform
Trike	Trichloroethylene
Trilene	Trichloroethylene
Trimethylbenzenes, all isomers or mixtures	Trimethylbenzenes, all isomers or mixtures
Tri-o-cresyl phosphate	Tri-o-tolyl phosphate
Triphenyl phosphate	Triphenyl phosphate
Tripoli, respirable dust	Silica, respirable crystalline
Trydimite, respirable dust	Silica, respirable crystalline
Tungsten & compounds (as W)	Tungsten & compounds (as W)
Turpentine	Turpentine
VCM	Vinyl chloride
Vinyl carbinol	Allyl alcohol
Vinyl chloride monomer	Vinyl chloride
Vinyl cyanide	Acrylonitrile
Vinylbenzene	Styrene
water-soluble nickel compounds	water-soluble nickel compounds
nickel and water-insoluble nickel compounds	nickel and water-insoluble nickel compounds
Wool process dust	Wool process dust
Xylol	Xylene, o-,m-,-p- or mixed isomers
Yttrium	Yttrium
Zinc chloride, fume	Zinc chloride, fume
Zinc distearate	Zinc distearate
Zirconium compounds (as Zr)	Zirconium compounds (as Zr)
α-Chlorotoluene	Benzyl chloride

References

1   *The Control of Substances Hazardous to Health (Amendment) Regulations 2004* SI 2004/3386 The Stationery Office 2004 ISBN 0 11 051407 6

2   *COSHH essentials: Easy steps to control chemicals. Control of Substances Hazardous to Health Regulations* HSG193 (Second edition) HSE Books 2003 ISBN 0 7176 2737 3 (a web version is available at www.coshh-essentials.org.uk)

3   *Control of Substances Hazardous to Health Regulations 2002* SI 2002/2677 The Stationery Office 2002 ISBN 0 11 042919 2

4   *Asthmagen? Critical assessments of the evidence for agents implicated in occupational asthma* HSE Books 1997 ISBN 0 7176 1465 4

5   *Control of substances hazardous to health. The Control of Substances Hazardous to Health Regulations 2002 (as amended). Approved Code of Practice and guidance* L5 (Fifth edition) HSE Books 2005 ISBN 0 7176 2981 3

6   *Monitoring strategies for toxic substances* HSG173 HSE Books 1997 ISBN 0 7176 1411 5

7   *The Data Protection Act 1998 Ch 29* The Stationery Office 1998 ISBN 0 10 542998 8

8   *List of MAK and BAT values: Maximum concentrations and biological tolerance values at the workplace* Deutsche Forschungsgemeinschaft Weinheim VCH Verlagsgesellschaft 2001 ISBN 3527275096

9   *TLSs and BEIs: Threshold limit values for chemical substances and physical agents and biological exposure indices* American Conference of Governmental Industrial Hygienists, Cincinnati, Ohio 2001 ISBN 1 882417 40 2

10   *Documentation of the threshold limit values and biological exposure indices* (Seventh edition) American Conference of Governmental IndustrialHygienists, Cincinnati, Ohio 2001 ISBN 888241743 7

11   *Summary criteria for occupational exposure limits* Environmental Hygiene Guidance Note (Loose leaf binder) EH64 HSE Books 2002 ISBN 0 7176 2569 9

12   *Approved supply list. Information approved for the classification and labelling of substances and preparations dangerous for supply. Chemicals (Hazard Information and Packaging for Supply) Regulations 2002. Approved list* L129 (Seventh edition) HSE Books 2002 ISBN 0 7176 2368 8

13   *General methods for sampling and gravimetric analysis of respirable and inhalable dust* MDHS14/3 (Third edition) HSE Books 2000 ISBN 0 7176 1749 1

14   *Determination of rubber process dust and rubber fume (measured as cyclohexane-soluble material) in air: Laboratory method using filters, gravimetric determination and soxhlet extraction* MDHS47/2 (Second edition) HSE Books 1999 ISBN 0 7176 2419 6

15   *Dust: General principles of protection* Environmental Hygiene Guidance Note EH44 (Third edition) HSE Books 1997 ISBN 0 7176 1435 2

16   *Approved classification and labelling guide. Chemicals (Hazard Information and Packaging for Supply) Regulations 2002. Guidance on Regulations* L131 (Fifth edition) HSE Books 2002 ISBN 0 7176 2369 6

17   *Control of Asbestos at Work Regulations 2002* SI 2002/2675 The Stationery Office 2002 ISBN 0 11 042918 4

18   *Asbestos: The analysts' guide for sampling, analysis and clearance procedures* HSG248 HSE Books 2005 ISBN 0 7176 2875 2

19   *A guide to the Asbestos (Licensing) Regulations 1983 as amended. The Asbestos (Licensing) Regulations 1983. Guidance on Regulations* L11 (Second edition) HSE Books 1999 ISBN 0 7176 2435 8

20   *Work with asbestos which does not normally require a licence. Control of Asbestos at Work Regulations 2002. Approved Code of Practice and guidance* L27 (Fourth edition) HSE Books 2002 ISBN 0 7176 2562 1

21   *Work with asbestos insulation, asbestos coating and asbestos insulating board. Control of Asbestos at Work Regulations 2002. Approved Code of Practice and guidance* L28 (Fourth edition) HSE Books 2002 ISBN 0 7176 2563 X

22   *The management of asbestos in non-domestic premises. Regulation 4 of the Control of Asbestos at Work Regulations 2002. Approved Code of Practice and guidance* L127 HSE Books 2002 ISBN 0 7176 2382 3

23   *Control of Lead at Work Regulations 2002* SI 2002/2676 The Stationery Office 2002 ISBN 0 11 042917 6

24   *Control of lead at work. Control of Lead at Work Regulations 2002. Approved Code of Practice and guidance* L132 (Third edition) HSE Books 2002 ISBN 0 7176 2565 6

25   *Preventing asthma at work. How to control respiratory sensitisers* L55 HSE Books 1994 ISBN 0 7176 0661 9

26   *Medical aspects of occupational asthma* Medical Guidance Note MS25 (Second edition) HSE Books 1998 ISBN 0 7176 1547 2

27   *Mines and Quarries Act 1954 Ch70* The Stationery Office 1954

28   *Coal Mines (Respirable Dust) Regulations 1975* SI 1975/1433 The Stationery Office 1975

29   *The Interdepartmental Group on Health Risks from Chemicals: First report and forward plan to 2002* Institute for Environment and Health, University of Leicester ISBN 1 899110 34 8

30   *Environmental Protection Act 1990 Ch43* The Stationery Office 1990 ISBN 0 10 544390 5

31   *Occupational exposure limits for hyperbaric conditions: Hazard assessment document* Environmental Hygiene Guidance Note EH75/2 HSE Books 2000
ISBN 0 7176 1899 4

32   *The safe use of pesticides for non-agricultural purposes. Control of Substances Hazardous to Health Regulations 1994. Approved Code of Practice* L9 (Second edition) HSE Books 1995 ISBN 0 7176 0542 6

33   *Code of Practice for the safe use of pesticides on farms and holdings* Under review (available free from Information Services Branch, Pesticides Safety Directorate, Mallard House, King's Pool, 3 Peasholme Green, York YO1 7PX
Tel: 01904 455733, or can be downloaded from: www.pesticides.gov.uk)

34   *Man-made mineral fibre: Airborne number concentration by phase-contrast light microscopy* MDHS59 HSE Books 1988 ISBN 0 7176 0319 9

35   *Biological monitoring in the workplace: A guide to its practical application to chemical exposure* HSG167 HSE Books 1997 ISBN 0 7176 1279 1

Printed and published by the Health and Safety Executive   04/05   C200